AMERICAN FADS

AMERICAN FADS

Richard A. Johnson

BTB
BEECH TREE BOOKS
A QUILL EDITION
New York

Grateful acknowledgment is made for permission to reprint lyrics from "The Ballad of Davy Crockett," copyright 1954 by Wonderland Music Co., Inc. Words by Tom Blackburn, music by George Bruns.

Library of Congress Cataloging-in-Publication Data

Johnson, Richard A. (Richard Alan), 1953–
  American fads.

  1. United States—Popular culture—History—20th century. 2. United States—Social life and customs—1971–   . I. Title.
E169.12.J643 1985   973.92   85–15670
ISBN 0-688-04903-6 (pbk.)

Printed in the United States of America

First Edition

1 2 3 4 5 6 7 8 9 10

BOOK DESIGN BY JAMES UDELL

The word "book" is said to derive from *boka,* or beech.
The beech tree has been the patron tree of writers since ancient times and represents the flowering of literature and knowledge.

To Dick and Rexetta

CONTENTS

INTRODUCTION

America likes to get crazy every now and then. Sometimes the country goes right off the deep end. But it is usually for a good cause—something like a Hula Hoop,® or a Slinky,® or the Twist, or the thrill of seeing how many college freshmen can be wedged into a telephone booth.

Nothing mobilizes the population like a big booming fad that comes bustin' out all over. Americans just love to latch on to the latest and the greatest no matter if it involves guzzling goldfish or stripping to the bare essentials and doing a mean streak. We're suckers for the next bit of nonsense to come sweeping down the plain. We turn ourselves into a coast-to-coast theater of the absurd every time someone creates a clever new plastic toy or thinks of a new way to wear blue jeans.

Just about anything can become a fad. It can be as ridiculous as a Pet Rock® or as ingenious as Rubik's Cube.® It can be a dance step, a doll, a pair of sunglasses, a toy, even a historical figure. About the only prerequisite is that it get from Long Beach to Long Island in a fortnight or less.

Fads are often blue sparks off the dynamo of youth. Most crazes start somewhere between kindergarten and college and then ooze into the adult world. A fad can originate at a ghetto high school in Philadelphia, in a Harvard dormitory room, or on a playground in southern California.

But though it may start with the young, a real fad can touch everyone's lives. Only a hermit hidden in a cave could have gotten through the summer of 1958 without someone dropping a Hula Hoop® over his head. And only a severe shut-in could have missed seeing a streaker in the spring of 1974.

Fads are about buying panics, cocksure instant tycoons, media blitzes, product spin-offs, and pseudointellectualizing. They are giant symbols for analysis. The Davy Crockett craze, said one psychologist, reflected the "need for disciplined exploration in literally hacking our way through the social frontiers." The Hula Hoop,® according to another, showed that "a child feels secure in a family circle." The Twist was "a proper cure for working off frustrations." Streaking was "an attack on dominant social values." The Pet Rock® caught on because "people were tired of all the gloom and wanted a good laugh." Cabbage Patch Kids™ appealed to "a universal need that children have to hold something and cuddle it."

A fad is a form of energy, like thunder and lightning, and it is just as hard to bottle. No one can mastermind a fad. It grows out of all proportion to marketing strategies or publicity campaigns. It takes on a life of its own, coursing through the veins of the country like a wonder drug.

Still, behind most fads there is an "only in America," entrepreneurial success story—overnight sensations like Slinky® inventor Richard James, Mood Ring king Joshua Reynolds, Pet Rock® star Gary Dahl, and Cabbage Patch creator Xavier Roberts.

This is the story of forty of the most famous American fascinations. They are rip-roarin' rages that made history and made people happy. Today, they are wonderful memories waiting to be refreshed.

SWALLOWING GOLDFISH

AP/Wide World Photos

Swallowing Goldfish

Joe College, 1939, was nothing like his boisterous boola boola brother from the twenties. He was a child of the Depression Era: purposeful, sober-minded, questioning values, contemplating war—and swallowing goldfish.

Indeed, there was nothing so sobering as watching a fellow student gulp a live specimen plucked from a bowl of goldfish. But then what better way to shed the weight of the world?

It was the first of the absurdist fads on campus, the forebear of phone booth stuffing, piano smashing, and dozens of other rituals of collegiate lunacy. It also remains the most famous and surely most amiably repulsive bit of campus madness ever concocted.

Harvard freshman Lothrop Withington, Jr., became the first to indulge on March 3, 1939. The son of a Boston lawyer and Harvard's 1919 football captain, he boasted about having once eaten a live fish during a bull session at Holworthy Hall. A fellow student offered him $10 to do it again and Withington agreed, assuring himself lasting fame by setting a time and place for the feat and allowing classmates to spread the word.

The dining hall at the Freshman Union was crowded, and cameras were popping when he grabbed a wiggling three-inch fish from a small bowl, held it by the tail, bent over backward until he faced the ceiling and lowered the fish into his mouth. Withington chewed, then swallowed hard—so did everyone else in the room.

He pulled a toothbrush from his pocket, cleaned his teeth, and remarked that "the scales caught a bit on my throat as it went down." Whereupon the freshman sat down to a meal of fried filet of sole with tartar sauce.

Word of Withington spread to Franklin and Marshall College in Lancaster, Pennsylvania, where three weeks later undergraduate Frank Hope, Jr., declared the Harvard man a "sissy" and outdid him by swallowing three goldfish. Hope added salt and pepper, but declined to chew—preferring to down the live fish with a quick guzzling technique.

But Hope's record lasted less than twenty-four hours. The next day another Franklin and Marshall student, George Raab, decided to "show Hope who's the sissy" and swallowed six fish.

With Hope and Raab's attack on the goldfish standard, the race was on. Harvard struck back with Irving Clark, Jr., who threw back two dozen and then took the stunt one step further by setting prices on various other indelicacies. He would eat almost any bug for a nickel, an angleworm for a dime, and a beetle for two bits.

Within a week after the Franklin and Marshall duo turned goldfish swallowing into an intercollegiate sport, dozens of other schools entered the competition. Gilbert Hollandersky of the University of Pennsylvania did Clark one better by swallowing twenty-five goldfish, then expunged the taste from his mouth with a steak dinner.

New records were reported almost every day. The University of Michigan's Julius Aisner downed twenty-eight, Donald V. Mulcahy of Boston College polished off twenty-nine, and Albright College football captain Michael Bonner ate thirty-three. Amid dozens of classmates and a small contingent of police officers, MIT freshman Albert Hayes signified his graduation year by gobbling forty-two fish.

The setting became almost as important as the fish count. Jack Smookler of Northeastern University digested thirty-eight fish outside Boston's Opera House while a small crowd looked on. Gordon Southworth, a veterinary student at Middlesex University, stomached sixty-seven while standing next to Soldier's Monument in Waltham Common. He pulled them one by one from a teeming pail and completed the task in fourteen minutes.

Clark University's Joseph Deliberato set a record that seemed destined to last when he swallowed eighty-nine at one sitting in early April. But occasional campus revivals—intended usually as nostalgic tributes—have produced new champions. By the 1970's the record for goldfish gluttony had surpassed three hundred.

The first co-ed to guzzle a live fish was Marie Hansen of the University of Missouri. But another female student, Betty Hines of Boston University, gained fame that spring by whipping up a goldfish sugar cookie with the chef at the Hotel Statler, who made it the week's special.

There was a variety of methods to the madness. While Withington actually sank his teeth into the fish, others did not. Hayes explained that "you lay the goldfish back on the tongue, let it wiggle till it hits the top of the throat, and then give one big gulp. Same effect as swallowing a live oyster."

Some used chasers. Mulcahy washed down his fish with three bottles of milk, while Hayes used four bottles of chocolate soda. Irving Clark sucked on an orange between each historic gulp.

Not everyone held the prank harmless. A Massachusetts state legislator introduced a bill that would "preserve the fish from cruel and wanton consumption." So incensed was the president of Boston's Animal League that he vowed to have the thrill seekers arrested if campus officials did not put a halt to goldfish swallowing. "This is not a subject for levity," he said. "I hesitate to bring such a matter to court, but we won't sidestep the issue. There have been too many complaints."

More threatening was word from a pathologist at the U.S. Public Health Service that goldfish may harbor disease or contain tapeworms that lodge in the intestine and cause the swallower to become anemic.

By late spring of 1939 the rate of goldfish gobbling finally let up, succumbing more to boredom than somber health warnings. But before the swallowing ceased, there flourished a general enthusiasm for unusual eats.

Unimpressed with "Eastern sissies," University of Chicago junior John Patrick bit into a phonograph record to prove his mettle. He chewed and swallowed two and one half Victrola discs before quitting, but declined to eat the labels. Meanwhile, word unfortunately filtered up from the University of Arkansas that a sophomore had bitten off the head of a king snake.

"The craving of these goldfish cultists really is for public acclaim, that is, exhibitionism," said Robert McMurray, a consulting psychologist from Chicago. "The eater of goldfish takes delight in the repulsiveness of the act."

Other professionals found goldfish swallowing akin to jitterbugging and urged parents and pedantics not to worry—for even fish too shall pass.

SLINKY®

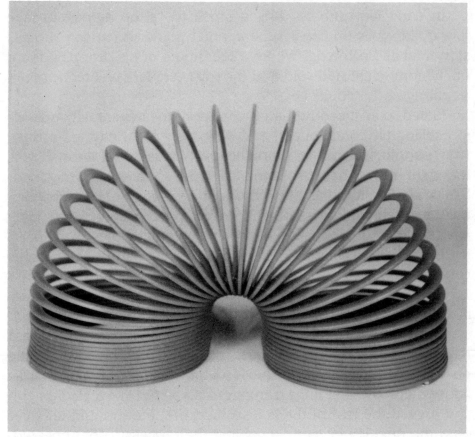

A twenty-six-year-old Philadelphia inventor named Richard James had stumbled onto one of the great toy gimmicks of all time—and he knew it.

But as he circulated his plaything among the city's major department stores in 1945, he could find none that would stock the unconventional item—a springy, spunky coil of flat-rolled wire.

James graduated from Penn State in 1939 and worked as a mechanical engineer in a shipyard during the war years. One day a large torsion coil in his office fell off a shelf and began to move as though springing to life. James immediately conceived of a toy and began developing the idea in his spare time. When James succeeded in charming a bedridden boy with his newly christened "Slinky," he arranged to have a few produced and began knocking on doors.

In early November 1945, a small toy shop agreed to take four dozen coils on consignment, and another American success story had its beginning. Within a few hours of his dropping them off, all forty-eight had sold and the toy merchant wanted more—as many as he could get.

Elated, convinced he had a winner, James eventually quit his job selling air conditioners, and with his wife, Betty, as a business partner, set out to manufacture Slinkies® full time. It was the right move because America was soon to go silly over Slinkies.® The toy was a 1945 Christmas-season hit in Philadelphia, and tens of thousands more were purchased in 1946. Only James's limited production capacity prevented sales from soaring even higher. They were toys, but grown-ups bought them as conversation springboards and objets d'light.

A Slinky® was eighty-seven feet of flat wire coiled into three-inch-diameter circles that stood less than two inches high when stacked. Its most famous trick was "walking" down stairs like a reluctant debutante. If properly positioned and given a little push, the amazing spring uncoiled and recoiled in a methodic goose step. The first rings clamped onto a step like a suction cup and tugged the rest of the coil so hard that the top end fell over onto the next lower step—enabling the process to be repeated.

Besides descending stairs, a Slinky® could be clasped at both ends and pulled open and closed as though shuffling cards or playing an accordion. The ends could be held in flat, up-turned palms and the Slinky® made to resemble churning pistons by alternately raising and lowering each hand. You could also "bounce" the toy by holding a few coils tightly in one hand, allowing the rest to hang down, and then moving the hand slowly up and down. In all its tricks the coil behaved as if made of muscle and fiber—a slithering metallic snake.

After the toy shop sold out of the first four dozen, James arranged to have them manufactured by a local piston-ring producer. He then placed the goods in Gimbels' Philadelphia store and demonstrated the toy himself.

While putting a Slinky® through its paces for an hour and a half, he sold four hundred at $1 each. Within a month, over twenty-five thousand had sold at Gimbels, prompting several other retailers to stock the hot coil. Eventually, stores in New York and elsewhere were selling Slinkies.® The young inventor and his James Industries were off and running.

Along the way he patented the idea, enabling him to fend off repeated attempts by others to market identical products. Even the piston-ring company he signed on came out with a replica, the Quirly.

James went to court to stop the Quirly and other Slinky® knockoffs and then began manufacturing the toy himself. Orders streamed in from all over the country, but a slew of problems befell the company after its initial sales burst. A steel shortage cut off supplies of flat-rolled wire, the company's lone distributor went bankrupt after losing $40,000 worth of Slinkies in a fire, and James got into a scrape with Philadelphia building inspectors he charged with soliciting bribes.

Production picked up again in 1948. The toy was caught in the postwar baby boom updraft and sales climbed during the fifties. Slinky® sales were soon setting new records and by 1953, James Industries was turning out seven thousand Slinkies® a day. Parents—who bought them in 1946 either as adolescents or young adults—were buying Slinkies for their kids. The earlier fad was regenerating itself.

Within a decade after James introduced his masterwork of amusement, an estimated fourteen million had sold. Indeed, they are still selling almost forty years after he first showed them to disinterested department store inventory buyers in Philadelphia.

There have been Slinky® "offspring" over the years, including a game that makes use of miniature coils and a plastic Slinky.® But the basic product has not changed since it was introduced.

Part of its enduring popularity stems from grown-up kids of the fifties who now buy Slinkies® for their own youngsters, figuring no American childhood could be complete without one. As such the Slinky® has become a shared experience, a rare link between generations.

SILLY PUTTY®

Binney & Smith, Inc.

General Electric wasn't sure what to make of—or make with—a laboratory discovery called "bouncing putty" that was introduced to the press in December 1944.

It was a chemical curiosity from a promising class of new materials known as silicones. It could be stretched and kneaded like taffy and broken into separate pieces if pulled suddenly. If rolled into a ball it would bounce like rubber, yet if left to stand, "bouncing putty" would gradually settle into a puddle.

Prospects for silicones were almost endless, and many product derivatives were already in practical use. But GE admitted that "bouncing putty," fascinating though it may be, had no known application. However, GE scientists were said to be still at work on the problem.

For a few weeks thereafter the futuristic substance was a small-scale novelty in Manhattan, where bits of it could be obtained in little cans. But the material was soon forgotten.

It might have remained forever an amusement for chemistry students had a thirty-six-year-old New Haven, Connecticut, entrepreneur named Peter Hodgson not happened onto a blob of the stuff five years later, in 1949.

Hodgson was shown a chunk of the "bouncing putty" that a chemist had left at the home of a mutual friend. He was instantly fascinated and noticed that others were too. After a few minutes of tugging on the lump of silicone, he began to consider its commercial possibilities.

At the time he was a down-on-his-luck ex-advertising copywriter who had recently been through a divorce. He'd been hired to produce a catalog for a New Haven toy shop, when he discovered the GE substance and decided to sell some of the material through the store.

The putty sold well and Hodgson later obtained a release from his employer, patented the name "SILLY PUTTY,®" and began marketing it himself. He purchased $150 worth of putty from General Electric and began breaking off one ounce dabs for sale.

He chose to encase the material in inexpensive plastic "eggs" out of economic necessity. But a few months later he told *The New Yorker,* "Easter eggs being so unimaginative, I decided to combine my putty with Easter and give them both a lift."

He promoted the peculiar properties of bouncing putty, but added one that General Electric had not talked about. When pressed against the color comic pages of a newspaper it would pick up a vivid reproduction. Once embossed on the elastic putty, the image could be stretched to hilarious extremes.

Hodgson, who said the material cost him $7 a pound, slapped a $1 price tag on each one-ounce unit and began taking his egg crates to retail outlets around the country. Neiman Marcus in Dallas bought some and so did the Doubleday bookshop in St. Louis.

SILLY PUTTY® sold so well in the St. Louis Doubleday store that the New York store ordered some. One day a writer from *The New Yorker* spotted the oddity for sale, interviewed Hodgson, and wrote almost a thousand words for the August 26, 1950 edition.

The article touched off a full-blown SILLY PUTTY® fad. Orders came in from all over the country, and Hodgson struggled to keep up. By late summer he had requests for a quarter of a million eggs, and the total approached one million by Christmas. The first radio commercial—on WQKR in New York—hailed "the biggest novelty fad in years."

It was America's sophisticated plaything in 1950—a fascinating blend of science and novelty that had everyone stretching and breaking and molding and bouncing, and best of all, picking up Dick Tracy from the Sunday funnies.

Silicone, a plastic substance refined from sand, provided great resistance to water and extreme temperatures. Silicone rubber, of which the putty was only one form, was used for gaskets on B-29 turbosuperchargers and to protect searchlight lenses from shocks. The putty version was a fundamentally worthless mascot for an important chemical blend that would yield numerous practical applications over the next forty years.

But Hodgson thought up ways to utilize the funny goop. Bedridden hospital patients could exercise their fingers and athletes could strengthen their wrists and forearms, he said. He urged neurotics to relieve tension by handling SILLY PUTTY® and pointed out that wobbly furniture could be leveled by inserting pieces under short table legs.

But the secret of SILLY PUTTY's® success was amusement and diversion, not utility. The mysterious and multifaceted compound took people's minds off "family difficulties" and Korea, Hodgson asserted.

By 1951, however, Korea was taking people's minds off SILLY PUTTY.® The onset of the war caused the government to place controls on certain defense-related material, including silicone, which could be used for making synthetic rubber. Although there was still demand for his product, Hodgson all but went out of business for lack of raw material.

After silicone was finally released for private industrial use, Hodgson virtually started from scratch to reestablish interest in the toy. In time, SILLY PUTTY® was revived, but kids rather than adults made up the customers of the future. By the mid-fifties, SILLY PUTTY® was sold in toy stores all over America to kids from "four to forever," as the modern packaging affirms. Hodgson's business grew to $5 million a year by 1960.

Ironically, Hodgson discouraged use of the material by children under seven at the height of the original craze. He worried that kids would swallow it, get it in their hair, or break it apart and scatter the pieces.

Four decades after General Electric introduced its freaky material, the SILLY PUTTY® package is still shilling the same bag of tricks. It "takes up comics in full color, then stretches them into something funnier . . . bounces higher than a rubber ball," and "lifts drawings and backward pencil writing for your own secret code."

SILLY PUTTY® has become a marvel of toy merchandising and part of the national vernacular. But no, General Electric never found a practical use for the stuff.

MODEL TRAINS

Model Railroader Magazine

Electric trains have been an American dream machine ever since 1900, when Joshua L. Cowen founded the Lionel Corporation and became pied piper to millions of kids. But it was in the years after World War II that model railroading really exploded—becoming THE toy for the baby boom boy.

Sales at Lionel had risen steadily in the years after the Depression and hit an all-time high in 1941, when the company switched to the production of war matériel. The legendary Cowen (his middle name was Lionel) bided his time turning out military hardware and planning brilliantly for the return of miniature railroading.

When the world came back from war, Lionel was ready with innovations like radio-wave transmitters, and real billowing smoke. The toy picked up full-throttle momentum and reached a state of fad merriment that peaked in 1952 and 1953 when Christmas mornings in America meant nothing if not a toy train under the tree.

Cowen, a tinkerer from his nineteenth-century boyhood, made his first mark in the world of gadgets at age eighteen. He patented a fuse to ignite photographer's flash powder and sold it to the Navy for detonating mines. Later, while experimenting with a dry-cell battery, he developed what many believe was the first flashlight. According to legend, Cowen was frustrated with the erratic portable light source and saw little practical use for it. He wound up turning the whole thing over to a business partner, Conrad Hubert, who started the Eveready Flashlight Company and amassed a huge fortune.

At age nineteen, while working in Manhattan, Cowen built his first toy train. It was an open wooden flatcar housing a small electric motor that ran on a track made of brass strips joined by wood ties. The first boom in electric train sales occurred in 1907 after Cowen replaced the wooden car with a model patterned after a real Baltimore and Ohio locomotive.

Buyers could augment the engine with numerous cars, including day coaches, cattle, coal and box cars, and cabooses. Over the next thirty years he added transformers, remote control, loading and unloading devices, and many more cars.

Sales continued to climb as Lionel emerged far and away as the leader of America's burgeoning toy train market. Only A. C. Gilbert Company, developer and marketer of the Erector Set, offered any serious competition in the realm of model railroading.

In 1941, volume hit a record $4.3 million, but war was at hand. Lionel dismantled its toy train assembly lines and signed contracts to produce gun mounts, fuse setters and dozens of other military goods. The contracts were canceled the day after an atom bomb leveled Hiroshima in August 1945, and Lionel went at breakneck pace to retool and rearm for the small train wars. The goal was to be back on track by Christmas, 1945.

Of course, Cowen and his slick team of inventors and engineers had lots up their sleeves. They came out of the gate with smoking smokestacks, whistling whistles, automatic and realistic coupling and loading, freight cars that dropped off cattle, tiny men who unloaded milk cans, and a detailed scale version of the steam turbine locomotive run by the Pennsylvania Railroad.

Not many train sets made it out the door in time for Christmas, but in 1946 both Lionel and A. C. Gilbert gathered a full head of steam. On June 5, 1946, Lionel threw a pre-Father's Day open house party for grown-ups only at its showrooms on Twenty-sixth Street in Manhattan.

The gimmick was golden. To be admitted to this showcasing of postwar innovations, adults had to bring along evidence of fatherhood.

It was a standard joke of the time. Toy railroads were for children, but dads loved them almost as much and would commandeer train sets purchased for the family small fry.

Over five hundred fathers showed up for the 1946 open house with birth certificates, maternity ward paperwork, photographs, crayon drawings of trains, folded diapers and pink baby socks. They got to see trains chug around a circuit set up with dazzling verisimilitude, including flashing signals, tunnels, bridges, lumber sheds, and cars that lifted freight with an electric magna-crane.

Such promotional genius, attracting fathers of the coming baby boom, helped pave the way for a meteoric surge in sales that mirrored the birth rate. Beginning in 1946, a steadily rising number of youngsters were growing into an age of train appreciation. Meanwhile, parents seemed only too happy to introduce young ones to the wonders of miniature passenger and freight lines that bore the insignias of real railways like Rock Island, Union Pacific, Baltimore and Ohio, and Lackawanna and Western.

It wasn't just fathers and sons who participated in the model-railroading craze. Numerous restaurants set up trains that ran along lunch counters carrying food orders to patrons. During a fundraising campaign at Pennsylvania Station in New York, contributions were deposited in a toy train car, which transported the coins and dumped them into a collection box by remote control.

Sales at Lionel quickly surpassed the prewar record, hitting the $10 million mark in 1946 and going over $21 million in 1950. The company experienced its greatest years early in the new decade, when toy trains became a symbol of the American family at ease and Joshua Lionel Cowen was proclaimed a national leisure-time hero.

Reader's Digest titled a biographical sketch "He Put Tracks Beneath the Christmas Tree," and *Newsweek* paid homage in a story in its December 29, 1952, edition—appearing just a few days after a Christmas season in which parents bought a record number of train sets.

It became clear three months into 1953 that yet another record year was in the offing. A short item appearing in *The New York Times* in March 1953, noted that "orders show a great increase in the demand for trains and accessories."

Citing Lionel president Lawrence Cowen, the son of the founder, the *Times* reported that "buyers who normally account for about 75 percent of the company's volume have already booked Lionel's planned production for the year." It was indeed a great year for model railroading in the United States, with sales at Lionel—the only toy manufacturer listed on the Big Board of the New York Stock Exchange—zooming past $30 million.

The apex of America's love affair with the Lilliputian tracks and trains was Christmas, 1953. Enthusiasm even spread to the White House, where Dwight and Mamie Eisenhower placed a Lionel set under the tree for grandson David.

But the nation's infatuation with toy trains began to wither in 1954. Two years after the high-water mark of 1953, sales had plunged over a third at both Lionel and A. C. Gilbert's American Flyer. Before the decade was out, the 1953 volume had been halved, and in 1963, model railroads were surpassed by another father and son sensation—motorized slot cars.

The glory days are gone, but toy trains have survived slot cars and other modern amusements that were supposed to derail them for good. The electric train is no longer a fad but remains part of the nation's pastime heritage.

3-D MOVIES

J. R. Eyerman, *Life* Magazine, 1952 Time Inc.

The movie audience that put on cardboard-frame, 3-D eyeglasses for the much-heralded world premiere of *Bwana Devil* in Los Angeles in November 1952, thought it was gazing into the future of cinema.

They were there to witness the first of the stereoscopic films, testing out a technology that many believed would revolutionize the industry in the same way that talkies had turned Hollywood on its ear.

The crowds that flocked to see *Bwana Devil* and other first-wave "deepies" were wonder-struck. By early 1953 some major studios were planning almost nothing but three-dimensional films, and most movie companies had at least one 3-D project in the works.

In the midst of a severe box office slump, Hollywood was pulling out all the stops to survive in the age of television. Technicolor was becoming standard, wide screen systems such as Cinerama and CinemaScope emerged, Stereophonic sound was added, and a technique called Smell-O-Vision was even installed in a few theaters.

But of all the innovation and gimmicks, 3-D was the most alluring and promising. It was a visual breakthrough, an enhancement of the theatergoing experience that could never be matched on the small screen.

Indeed, for several months the 3-D process known as Natural Vision was the brightest star in Hollywood, a name above the title that was pure magic. Yet unlike most of the new technology and theatrical aids, stereoscopy failed to survive. The novelty wore off so fast that by 1954, films shot in 3-D had to be released in flat form or risk box office disaster.

Three-dimensional movies were really nothing new in 1952. The small visual trick had been around since the turn of the century, yet there were only minimal improvements in the basic technology over fifty years—a fact which was widely blamed for the failure of 3-D in the fifties.

Three-dimensional processes were patented in the United

States, Great Britain, and France around 1900; but there was little commercial application until twenty years later. Several 3-D films were successfully presented in Europe during the twenties, but interest receded with the emergence of sound.

Experimentation continued in Europe and the United States during the thirties, and the first Polaroid glasses were used by audiences at a special exhibit at the New York World's Fair in 1939. A color stereoscopic process making use of spectacles and a polarized filter on the projector proved to be one of the most popular stops at the fair—an indication of the 3-D hysteria that would strike American movie houses thirteen years later.

Television was thought to be the reason for a sharp decline in movie ticket sales in the early fifties, and the future of the industry seemed in doubt. The studios went into a crisis mode, cutting back on planned releases and driving thousands of actors, directors, producers, writers, and technicians either into television or onto the unemployment line.

A great shakeout that would dwarf the move from silence to sound a quarter century earlier was widely predicted. The only way the industry could survive would be to accentuate the contrast with TV—to create a new sense of visual awe to rival the intimacy of television.

Among the wraparound wide-screen processes trotted out by studios were Cinerama, CinemaScope, VistaVision, Superama, Glamarama, Todd-A-O, Warnerscope, and Magna Screen. The idea was to expand the field of vision, making the movie experience more like the Broadway spectacle. The filming of such sprawling theatrical hits as Rodgers and Hammerstein's *Oklahoma!* was among the first projects planned for a wide cinematic scope.

Stereophonic sound, which was used brilliantly in Walt Disney's *Fantasia* several years earlier, became more commonplace, and there were suddenly more films made in color than black and white.

But it was stereoscopic vision that was supposed to knock TV out of the box. At least that is what most studio executives believed after the first Natural Vision release, the modestly budgeted and poorly scripted *Bwana Devil,* opened to packed houses in Los Angeles on November 26, 1952.

Whatever doubts there were about the commercial applicability of 3-D were swept away with the success of *Bwana Devil*. The movie was irresolutely panned by critics, but its dazzling new effect held everyone agog.

The film about a pair of man-eating lions that attack railroad construction crews in Africa grossed $95,000 during a record-breaking first week at a Los Angeles theater. Lines outside extended for two blocks as crowds waited to make a spectacle of themselves by wearing ill-fitting glasses and throwing their hands up when the man-eaters appeared to jump off the screen and into their laps. *Bwana Devil* wound up grossing about $5 million in the months after its release, putting it in a class with some of Hollywood's most profitable films.

The 3-D process used in *Bwana Devil* was a simulation of normal two-eyed vision. Horizontally separated lenses on the camera each represented the sight of one eye. When the two films were projected simultaneously in a theater, the polarized glasses drew them together to create the three-dimensional illusion.

Part of the gimmick was the glasses themselves. At first the mere act of putting on special Polaroid frames to watch a movie was exciting. A famous *Life* magazine photo of the futuristic-looking *Bwana Devil* premiere audience was a national curiosity. The strange vision of an audience from outer space helped fuel the 3-D fad and pave the way for the success of upcoming Natural Vision releases.

Movies shot in stereoscopy played for 3-D effect. An endless stream of guns, knives, scissors, fists, pitchforks, vicious animals, and monsters was thrust at the camera; audiences instinctively reared back. There were also subtler benefits, including a more lifelike presentation of the human figure. Ann Miller, wearing skintight pants for the "Too Darn Hot" number from *Kiss Me Kate*, became something of a 3-D pinup.

In the wake of *Bwana Devil* came Warner Brothers' *3-D House of Wax*, starring Vincent Price. It was the first major studio production to be released in stereoscope, and, like *Bwana Devil*, did boffo business. *House of Wax* was a better indication of how the process could be used to enhance the artistic value of a film and was such a huge success that Warner Brothers rashly announced that almost all its films would thereafter be released in 3-D.

Other studios were more cautious, but soon all had 3-D movies in production. However, by the end of summer, 1953, resistance to the new process had begun to take shape. The first dozen or so stereoscopic films were money-makers, but as audience complaints mounted, studios began to circulate more flat prints of 3-D films.

There was grumbling about headaches caused by projection of dual images out of synch and a growing dislike of the glasses needed to complete the 3-D effect. Cardboard specs became a nuisance outweighing the novelty of three-dimensional images on the screen. Meanwhile, no practical system existed for projecting stereoscopic imagery without Polaroid lenses.

Despite rapidly declining interest, many Hollywood studios had made too big a commitment to change gears quickly. Metro-Goldwyn-Mayer went ahead with both 3-D and standard versions of *Kiss Me Kate* in the winter of 1953–54. Alfred Hitchcock's *Dial M for Murder, Money from Home* with Dean Martin and Jerry Lewis, and *Miss Sadie Thompson,* starring Rita Hayworth, were all pegged for 3-D release by Columbia, but the studio decided to offer exhibitors conventional prints as well.

By the time all three were finally released in mid–1954, audience resistance had won out. Three-dimensional prints were locked away in studio vaults and forgotten about. The unreleased 3-D version of *Dial M for Murder* was discovered in 1980 and placed in a few theaters, where it was enthusiastically received. *Village Voice* film critic Andrew Sarris even chose the 3-D *Dial M* as his favorite "new" release of 1981.

But in 1954 audiences were only too happy to shed the silly glasses and get back to conventional movies. Three-D was perhaps a good idea, but its time most certainly had not come.

Burt Glinn, Magnum Photos, Inc.

American Fads

DAVY CROCKETT

When a new elementary school being built in Mansfield, Ohio, in 1955 lacked a name, the local board of education polled its future students for their choice. The winner: "Davy Crockett."

The board didn't take the kids' suggestion, but how fitting it would have been if they had. Davy Crockett, after all, was the first great hero of the postwar baby boom generation whose vast numbers made so many new school buildings necessary.

He was the supremely merchandisable King of the Wild Frontier, a legend in his own time and again in 1955. When Fess Parker first played the character on television, the nation's youth was entranced. There was a sudden and manic appreciation for a man who had died almost one hundred twenty years earlier at the Battle of the Alamo.

But the Crockett phenomenon was not so improbable as it seemed. Magnified by television, the colonel was an authentic image of America's frontier past. He was the two-fisted hero of an emerging superclass of children able to influence their parents' new spending power in ways yet undreamed of by toy manufacturers and entrepreneurs.

An audience of forty million watching TV's "Disneyland" on the night of Wednesday, December 15, 1954, saw the lanky twenty-nine-year-old Parker step into the Crockett persona for the first time. With his coonskin cap, buckskin clothes, and Tennessee drawl, he captivated the five-to-fifteen-year-olds who made up the largest share of the audience. But it was not Parker who became the phenomenon: It was the Crockett legend. Kids were overcome by the folksy yet bigger than life hero put before them.

Crockett was a classic overnight sensation, but it took a few weeks for manufacturers to catch up. They finally responded with a mammoth assortment of frontier regalia, as dozens of companies contributed to the estimated five hundred Crockett items that wound up on store shelves.

Among the most popular items were coonskin caps (the wholesale price of raccoon skins jumped from twenty-five cents a pound to eight dollars a pound), fringed buckskin clothing, toy powderhorn rifles, and moccasins.

But the toy industry, led by the merchandising division of Walt Disney Productions, wasn't stopping there. The Crockett line also included school lunch boxes, bathing suits, guitars, T-shirts, sweat shirts, bath towels, telephone sets, sleds, blankets, snow suits, plastic ice cream cones, and toothbrushes. There were also about fourteen million Davy Crockett books sold to both children and adults.

Probably the most popular item was Bill Hayes's recording of "The Ballad of Davy Crockett," an item which undoubtedly still rings in the ears of youngsters old enough to spin records on portable players in 1955:

> Davy, Daaaaaa-vy Crockett
> King of the Wild Frontier

It told a story of a brave backwoodsman, "born on a mountaintop in Tennessee," who "kilt a b'ar" at the age of three. Hayes's record was one of the biggest hits of all time. For five consecutive weeks, beginning March 26, "The Ballad of Davy Crockett" was listed as the No. 1 recording in the country by *Billboard* magazine. It sold an estimated four million copies and was translated into sixteen languages.

All told it is believed that $100 million in sales of Crockett-related items were rung up in 1955—making it the most commercially successful fad to date.

Retailers were awestruck. Nothing had ever carried the financial clout of Davy Crockett: not Zorro, not the Lone Ranger, not Superman or Mickey Mouse. It was the first flexing of the baby boom's financial muscle. A spokesman for a major New York department store called it "the boom that mushroomed."

To be sure, Disney cashed in, but the studio did not enjoy an exclusive copyright on Davy Crockett the historical character. As a result, numerous manufacturers took part in the deluge of products and divided up the considerable spoils.

But the Crockett craze was something more than a sellathon. The old frontiersman's sudden and spectacular eminence was played out in every setting, from school playgrounds to the halls of Congress.

But who *was* Davy Crockett and why did everyone take such a shine to him? He was born in 1786 and became a farmer, hunter, and pioneer in the development of western Tennessee. He scouted for Andrew Jackson in the Creek War and was a colonel in the Tennessee militia. After serving in the state legislature and three terms in Congress, he joined the Texans in their war against Mexico in 1835. He was one of 187 soldiers who made a heroic last stand at the Alamo, which was under attack by the Mexican general Santa Anna.

Though Davy Crockett's achievements stood out in an age of bravery, it was homespun wisdom and colloquial charm that solidified his place in American folklore. Among "Davyisms" found in numerous attributed writings are *ripsnorter, roughneck,* and *hard row to hoe.* Many of the forty or so *Crockett Almanacs* that appeared throughout the 1830's are believed to have been ghostwritten. But authentic or not, the language was enriched by works appearing under his name, and Americans in 1955 delighted in recycling some of his best down-home phrasemaking.

Crockett rose to such heroic dimensions that members of Congress in 1955 took to debating the whereabouts of his birth. Texans called him a favorite son for his brave deeds in the war against Mexico, and Tennessee Congressmen claimed him as a native. However, the North Carolina delegation noted that when Crockett was born on August 17, 1786, Tennessee was not a state, but part of a territory that comprised the State of North Carolina.

The Associated Press ran a story on the date of his birth, datelined Knoxville, Tennessee, pronouncing, "Exactly 169 years ago today he was born on a mountaintop in Tennessee."

When a group of schoolchildren visited Congress's Statuary Hall in June, they looked first for a monument of Crockett and thought they'd found it when they spotted the likeness of Dr. Marcus Whitman, an ex-pioneer of the Great Northwest, wearing buckskins and posed with coonskin cap and rifle. He was Davy to youngsters who passed through the hall that year. Adults let them believe rather than try to explain why such a great American hero did not have a statue of his own.

Part of the fun was trying to explain the Crockett craze. A family relations specialist, Dr. Evelyn Mills, saw a "need for disciplined exploration in literally hacking our way through the social frontiers." Crockett, she said, offered "tangible evidence of human beings able to battle the problems of their time."

Dr. Harold Greenwald, a New York psychologist who did consulting work for the toy industry, said children feel powerless to cope with the world, so they seek to identify with someone who seems able to control his world.

The waning of enthusiasm for Crockett began with the debunking of his legend. An article in *Harper's* depicted him as something of a louse, who had "weaseled his way out of the Army by hiring a substitute." Other irreverent accounts painted him as a drunkard, carouser, and surprisingly less than honest politician.

The deflation of Crockett's image may have had less to do with the fad's demise than the inflation of Crockett products in the marketplace. There were also widespread reports that coonskin caps made of imitation fur were highly flammable. An autumn pall fell over the retail sensation, and there was only a wisp of a fad left by the Christmas season.

Department stores drastically reduced the amount of counter space devoted to Crockett paraphernalia. The price of Davy Crockett T-shirts wilted from $1.29 to 39 cents, and, with coonskin cap orders being canceled by the hundreds of thousands, the fur market collapsed. *Variety* announced that "Davy was the biggest thing since Marilyn Monroe and Liberace, but he pancaked. He laid a bomb."

FRISBEE®
DISC

Dan Poynter. Reprinted from the *Frisbee Players' Handbook*, with permission

Frisbee® discs have been streaming back and forth between millions of Americans since 1957, when the now world-famous derivative of a pie pan became a national fad.

A year before Wham-O® Manufacturing Company rolled out the Hula Hoop,® the fabled California toymaker unveiled its first flying disc. The plastic dinner-sized plates made by Wham-O® and other manufacturers soared in popularity, but were overshadowed by the Hoop in 1958.

Of course, the Frisbee® disc has thrived long after the original sales boom. It was kept alive as a college boy's toy, saucering through the air on thousands of campus quadrangles since catching on with Ivy Leaguers in the spring of 1957.

The spinning aerodynamo appealed to thoughtful young men. It was a ponderer's plaything, a plastic device with a gift of flight that seemed borrowed from nature. Indeed, by the late 1960's, Frisbeeing had evolved into an organized sport on campus.

The joy of whirling a plastic disc across an expanse and into supple hands is hardly a mystery. But at least a small part of the allure in 1957 has been attributed to a national fascination in the fifties with "unidentified flying objects."

Americans might have seen more than a toy when a Frisbee® disc swooped toward them. A UFO skywatch mentality had taken hold in the days of the U.S. Air Force's Project Blue Book, and the plastic disc seemed like a pretty good depiction of how an invader craft ought to look. The implement was widely referred to as a "flying saucer" in those days, and the tag didn't wear off altogether until the early seventies.

The scientific principle behind the disc was simple. Airfoil causes lift and spinning gives gyrostability in flight. If thrown properly, with a sharp backhand flip of the wrist, the slender plate rifled toward the target at high speed, yet could be comfortably plucked from the air with one hand.

The disc could be lofted fifty or sixty yards before settling into a waiting palm. Snaring a long winding toss, which spun back toward the thrower in a near boomerang effect, required instinctive calculations based on speed and trajectory. An experienced player zeroed in on the right spot at the right time and took delivery of a flying disc that appeared destined to land several yards away.

Such were the delights of the toy, as thousands had discovered while spearing and chucking airworthy tin pans used by the Frisbie Baking Company of Bridgeport, Connecticut. According to some reports, the pie plates had been thrown for decades at nearby Yale University, but the cult came alive elsewhere after World War II. A Frisbie official estimated that the company lost about five thousand pie plates in the late forties to customers who failed to return them.

A California carpenter and building inspector named Fred Morrison first conceived of the pie plate's commercial possibilities. With a friend, Warren Francioni, he improved the pie-pan design, made a few metal prototypes, and in 1948 fashioned the first plastic disc by hand.

Morrison obtained a patent and in 1955 sold it to Wham-O®, a San Gabriel, California, company named after its first product, a heavy-duty slingshot. Wham-O® introduced a now legendary version of Morrison's design called the Pluto Platter®, which sold for fifty-nine cents.

Other manufacturers turned out plastic discs under names like "Scalo," "Space Saucer," and "Flying Saucer." Frisbee (the spelling of the bakery's name was altered) was a generic term that took root among Ivy League schools and was not acquired and trademarked by Wham-O® until 1959.

Collegians were once again first in line as the 1957 fad took off. The toy even took some credit for preventing a repeat of the campus rioting that occurred at several Eastern schools in the spring of 1956. But the appeal of the Frisbee® disc soon went beyond college students. By summer they were gliding, dipping, and sideslipping on beaches all over the country.

The greatest flying-saucer tossers in the world that year were said to have been on the beach at Waikiki, where vacationing engineers—fascinated by the plastic bird in flight—stood at water's edge and flung them majestically in the shadow of Diamond Head.

Though viewed as a novelty in 1957, within a decade the toy was enjoying a sporting afterlife as plenty of people began taking the old dish seriously. Much of the credit was given to Wham-O® Vice-President and General Manager Ed Headrick, who in the early sixties organized the International Frisbee® Association to sanction competition.

The U.S. Navy began experimenting with Wham-O® Frisbee® discs in 1968 to find a way to keep flares and other payload aloft longer. Since some practiced college kids could keep a plastic disc in the air for more than ten seconds, the Navy reasoned that a spinning platter might be used to illuminate targets for longer periods than traditional flares.

But navy engineers found that a weighted disc would not soar. There could be no tampering with the aerodynamic purity of the old pie plate as modified by Fred Morrison.

Meanwhile, fanatics turned their attention to serious sport. By the early seventies, intercollegiate Guts Frisbee® competitions were popular. The name dated back to 1957, when a few hearty

Princeton men threw not a plastic saucer, but a rusty six-inch circular-saw blade. The new Guts Frisbee® referred to flipping a disc in such a way that an opponent standing fifteen yards away could not catch it. To make it tough, the Frisbee® disc was thrown at eye-popping speed or with unusual spin or trajectory. A popular trick was to fling the thing at a 45-degree angle into the ground so that it would bounce back into level flight.

Thirty-six teams from several countries arrived at Copper Harbor, Michigan, in the summer of 1972 to take part in the World Guts Frisbee® Championships. But the game was replaced a few years later by more creative competitive spin-offs.

By 1975, the main game was Ultimate Frisbee,® in which teams moved up and down fields of play, sending the disc to one another and trying to zip it into an "end zone" before the saucer was dropped, intercepted, or flung out of bounds.

At about the same time, Wham-O® began putting on World Frisbee® Disc Championships that included everything from distance throwing and catching to Frisbee® disc versions of tennis, golf, gymnastics, and dance. There was even a dog catch competition in which contestants snatched far-flung Frisbee® discs in their mouths.

The phenomenon has gone on and on. Enthusiasts are still devising new ways to enjoy the toy—now offered in a variety of sizes and models—and the range of skill is forever increasing. With more than 100 million Wham-O® Frisbee® discs sold, the fad has become an institution.

HULA HOOP®

Courtesy of Kransco

No sensation has ever swept the country like the Hula Hoop.® It was the Great Obsession of 1958; the Waldorf Hysteria; the undisputed granddaddy of American fads.

The hoop rewrote toy merchandising history during the summer of that recession-bound year, and more than a quarter century later remains the one standard against which all national crazes are measured.

Simple strips of polyethylene tubing formed into circles and held together by a wooden plug and staples became a national pastime. The country seemed lost in a strange hoop-notic trance—women and children first, then dad, coaxed from his easy chair to give the hoop a whirl.

At its peak, literally dozens of manufacturers were into the swing of things. Everyone from radio and television personality Art Linkletter, who with partners opened nine hoop factories, to major oil companies supplying the petroleum-based plastic was on the bandwagon. Plastic extruders stopped making cable covering, piping, and garden hose and turned instead to more profitable hoops.

As fast as tubing could be squeezed out of converted machinery, it was shipped off under a variety of brand names to impatient retailers. By the fall of 1958, four months after the fad took hold, it was widely estimated that 25 million had sold at well over $30 million retail. And hoops continued to wrack up sales long after the novelty had worn off. Within a few years of their introduction, sales reached 100 million.

At the height of the hoop sensation, the Toy News Bureau reported that twenty-seven manufacturers were turning them out under such names as "Spin-A-Hoop," "Wiggle-A-Hoop," "Hoop-Zing," "Hooper Dooper," and "Whoop-De-Do." The original maker, Wham-O® Corporation, produced "Hula Hoops,®" but never cornered the market. Imitators exploited the company's weak patent position and flooded the nation with their hoops.

It hardly mattered, though, since Wham-O® was stretched to the limits of its production capacity during the peak months. Its San Gabriel installation was rolling out twenty thousand hoops a day and still falling behind orders.

The trick was to spin the hoop around the waist with a gentle swaying of the hips. One company's hoop came with a breezy set of instructions: "Hug the hoop to the backside . . . Push hard with the right hand . . . now rock, man, rock . . . don't twist . . . swing it . . . sway it . . . you got it."

The younger and more agile you were the better you could work the thing. A swivel-hipped ten-year-old managed ten thousand spins at a Hula Hoop® Derby at the Brookside Swim Club in New Jersey. But most adults moved stiffly from side to side while the hoop dropped to the floor.

There were other uses. You could jump through hoops while they rolled along the ground or toss them in a pool and dive inside the circle. They could be twirled about the neck, skipped through like a jump rope, or flung with a boomerang effect.

The fad started out west in the spring of 1958. Wham-O® founders Arthur Melin and Richard Knerr, having heard about gym classes in Australia where kids exercised enthusiastically with bamboo hoops, decided to produce a plastic version for sale in the United States.

They went to the polymer chemical division of W. R. Grace and Company for technical assistance and came up with the right plastic composition. Chemists developed an improved form of polyethylene called Grex, which had high tensile strength, was not affected by temperature changes, and would float, so that the hoop could be used for water games.

Once Wham-O® began manufacturing Hula Hoops,® Melin personally demonstrated the toy at playgrounds throughout southern California. Local kids bought thousands of them, and from there hoops spread overland overnight. It became one of the first trends to make an eastward sweep of the country—a route almost all fads now take.

By July, Wham-O® was in production full tilt, and dozens of other novelty-makers soon fell in line. Department stores staged demonstrations and offered free hoop lessons, but they hardly needed to bother. The craze was ablaze in every nook and cranny of the USA. One ecstatic hoop dealer declared, "It's bigger than Davy Crockett, bigger than Zorro, bigger than anything that ever hit the toy business."

The fanaticism knew no international bounds. So entranced were British subjects that newspapers in England devoted whole pages to hoop instructions and television stations broadcast live demonstrations.

The hoop reached Japan via newsreel and quickly became a national preoccupation. According to a newspaper dispatch from Tokyo in the fall of 1958, "every yard, vacant lot and alley is a potential site of a demonstration, and the practitioners are by no means all children."

The "huru hoopu," as it translated, also caused a furor in the Land of the Rising Sun. A young girl was killed while chasing her hoop into traffic, and many adults began complaining of slipped discs and disjointed backbones. By late November, police had banned them from the streets of Tokyo.

In contrast, hoops were usually portrayed in the United States as a wholesome way for adults to shake off a few pounds and promote overall good health. Yet a bevy of opinion-givers saw them as more than mere playthings. Some read a sexual motif into the faintly suggestive hip shake. Others pegged it as gentle rebellion—kids simply wanted to show up their parents by out-hooping them. Dr. Joyce Brothers, having just catapulted to fame by winning $134,000 on a television quiz show, surmised that "children evidently delight in the fact that they can keep the hoops spinning in orbit, while many adults can't."

A prominent New York psychiatrist speculated that hoops found favor because kids like circles. They draw rounded shapes when they are very young, they play ring-around-the-rosy, they feel secure in the family circle. Everyone had a theory for the hoop's success, or else grasped at larger meanings. With tongue in cheek, the amused *Wall Street Journal* suggested that it symbolized the Federal Reserve's well-rounded policies or else the promises of political office-seekers, with no beginning, middle, or end.

It was easier to explain why the hoop craze began to wilt in October. America had been saturated. Unlike the Davy Crockett boom three years earlier, which spawned some five hundred novelties for sale, the hoop had only the hoop, and the nation had its bellyful of them.

They originally sold for almost $3 retail, but by early fall they could be found in stores for as little as 50 cents apiece. Sales declined everywhere at once. Orders were canceled as frantically as they had been placed, and manufacturers scrambled for ways to keep the fad alive. There were suddenly multicolored hoops, hoops with bells, a distorted hoop that swung up and down, a hoop made of welded aluminum tubing, and a do-it-yourself hoop that allowed youngsters to fit various colored interlocking pieces together to form a circle.

Phillips Petroleum, which sold polyethylene to hoop makers, issued a circular to customers suggesting new uses. Phillips proposed a hoop equipped with a T-square handle to roll it along the ground, and a hoop with a rope lariat attached so it could be used as a leash for pets. If all else failed, Phillips advised makers to punch holes in hoops and sell them as lawn showers.

After trying unsuccessfully to revive the mania in 1964, Wham-O® did manage to score again with the hoop in 1967. The fabled toy maker did it by inserting five steel ball bearings in the plastic tubes to produce a "shoop-shoop" sound as the toy rotated. Several million "shoop-shoop" hoops sold for $1.98 apiece with the aid of an extensive television advertising campaign.

Though sales came nowhere near the level of a decade earlier, the company did a better job of covering what market there was. With patent secure, the second go-round was Wham-O's® alone.

Even hoop contests returned, but, for the most part, Americans in the late 1960's saw the toys as objects of nostalgia. Hula Hoops® were back, but they would never be the same.

Joe Munroe, *Life* Magazine, 1959 Time Inc.

American Fads

PHONE BOOTH PACKING

They were dubbed "The Silent Generation," but college students in the 1960's were a capering, free-spirited bunch who picked up where prewar goldfish swallowers left off.

True enough, fifties undergraduates were upright, career-directed, political care-nothings; but they also tended to lose control each spring when the weather turned warm. It was the age of frivolity on campuses across the country, and the national eye was focused on one ridiculous rite of spring after another. An era of crazy stunts culminated in the spring of 1959 with the most famous of all—phone booth cramming.

The madness had roots in the goldfish gobbling of the spring of 1939—the archetypal college loony binge that started at Harvard and within a few weeks had kids out West biting off the heads of king snakes.

Campus nonsense was at a minimum during the war years, and in the late 1940's colleges were dominated by serious-minded ex-servicemen going to school on the G.I. Bill. But the fifties ushered in a new inanity.

The pranks began at the University of Michigan in the spring of 1952 with the panty raid, a female undergarment obsession that took hold all across the country. Male students arrived in packs at the foot of women's dormitories and proceeded to climb to the balconies on trellises and ladders they had carted along. Co-eds-in-waiting responded either with panties or pails of water meant to cool off the marauders.

Panty raids were back again in the spring of 1953 and reappeared sporadically throughout the remainder of the decade. Nostalgic raids are still occasionally organized, but in an age of coeducational dorms, there is not the same excitement.

In the spring of 1955 students crammed themselves into small sports cars and then twelve months later turned into grandscale practical jokesters. They hoisted cars onto the roofs of college presidents' houses, tarred and feathered statues of university founders, flushed upper-floor toilets in dormitories in unison to flood the first floor, and filled the beds of unsuspecting classmates with goats, turtles, lizards, snakes, and pet alligators.

In 1957, students staged waterfights, threw plastic Frisbees® for the first time, and set endurance records for teeter-tottering and dribbling basketballs. A year later, hundreds of thousands descended on Fort Lauderdale during spring break to jump fully clothed into motel pools and generally create havoc.

The decade of friskiness finally peaked with the phone booth fill-ups of spring, 1959. Cramming caught on in the United States after a South African college sent word that it had set a "world record" by fitting twenty-five students into telephone quarters built for one. Next, a group of London University students packed into one of the wide-body British phone booths, but could fit no more than nineteen and fell short of the South Africans.

By early March, the fad had hit North America, and jam sessions were under way on several U.S. and Canadian campuses. Thousands of college kids were going nose to nose, ankle to earlobe, in rollicking competition. They were encased in glass for posterity—a classic picture of frenzied youth.

Most used upright, outdoor booths, but a few piled into prone booths as though getting into a boat. At a junior college in Modesto, California, students put a booth donated by the phone company on its side and went thirty-four high, claiming a new record. But others cried foul, arguing that only vertical hutches qualified.

Some loaded up in extra-large fraternity hall phone cubicles or other oversized units. But most participants insisted on standard American booths—disallowing the claim of forty Canadian boys who crammed into a compartment measuring four feet square and ten feet high on the Calgary campus of the University of Alberta.

One of the British rules required that someone in the booth either place a call or answer a ringing phone. Sticklers demanded that, once loaded up, the door be closed, while other cramming referees let hands and feet dangle outside.

At first, kids scrambled willy-nilly—as if cramming wadded paper into a drawer. But as the days of the craze went by, stuffers became sophisticated. Students at Ryerson Tech in Toronto stacked themselves sandwich-style, but their protruding legs caused pooh-poohing on other campuses when pictures came over the wire.

At MIT, students took a "scientific" approach—seating nineteen carefully and comfortably in a fraternity phone cubicle that was much larger than a public booth. "Here we think and calculate about the job," announced an MIT packager. "The mathematics of it are challenging."

But the most efficient packing was at St. Mary's College in Moraga, California, where twenty-two smallish undergraduates maneuvered into a booth with a well-planned and perfectly executed crosshatch stacking technique.

Onlookers encouraged the St. Mary's lads to "Beat South Africa" and later carted the rumpled, slightly compacted competitors around campus on their shoulders.

The fad continued into April with a few new wrinkles. Seven young men from Fresno College jammed into a booth sunk in a swimming pool, only to have their underwater record eclipsed by eight co-eds in the Fresno Hacienda Motel pool.

Some phone-boothing was combined with fraternity hazing. Upperclassmen usually organized crams and frequently "elected" small-bodied, uninitiated freshmen to wedge into booths.

The fad expired—as the world knew it would—when cramming for May and June final exams took precedence. When the stuffing stopped it marked the end of an era—the last gasp of a frivolous decade on campus. It was time to make room for the sixties.

THE TWIST

Michael Ochs Archives

Ground zero for the Twist—the original "dance sensation that swept the nation"—was the Peppermint Lounge on West Forty-fifth Street in New York City.

On a given night in 1961, with Joey Dee and the Starlighters onstage, the likes of Judy Garland, Tennessee Williams, the Duke and Duchess of Windsor—even Greta Garbo—could be seen leering at twisters or else trying out the kicky, suggestive new dance themselves.

Café society had come out for the Twist, turning it into an

international phenomenon. A fashion industry grew up around the dance, twist records by numerous artists climbed the charts, and a spate of twist movies played to packed houses.

Everyone, everywhere, was insisting on twisting. It became a daring symbol of a new era—one in which you danced with raw abandon and without touching your partner. It was welcome to the sixties, buddy, and fasten your seat belt.

The step had been popular with young blacks for several years—ever since veteran rhythm and blues artist Hank Ballard wrote and recorded "The Twist" in the mid-fifties. The song was a hit in the restricted R and B market, but white audiences were not exposed to it until 1960, when a nineteen-year-old ex-chicken plucker from Philadelphia named Ernest Evans recorded Ballard's song. On September 19, the new version zoomed to No. 1 on *Billboard* magazine's popular music charts and the fad was launched.

Evans had picked up a stage name when *American Bandstand* host Dick Clark pointed out his resemblance to pop music star Fats Domino. As the dance craze spread from black high school dances in South Philly to every sock hop in the country, the newly christened Chubby Checker rode the Twist to fame and fortune.

As teen dance fads went, the Twist was a simple maneuver. You either made like you'd just stepped out of the tub and were toweling off your back, or pretended to be stubbing out a cigarette butt on the floor with your big toe.

Dancers were apt to alternately squat and rise while twisting. In one variation, partners pretended to scratch their backs by moving up and down against an imaginary pillar. Another favorite was the "oversway," in which the twisting girl leaned backward while the boy stretched forward simultaneously.

The Twist was not difficult to master and not especially pleasing to the eye. Yet it revolutionized the dance floor and paved the way for more overtly erotic, expressionistic dances, rather than continuing offshoots of basic Jitterbug steps.

But the most popular dance since the Lindy Hop of the 1930's was already waning when the Peppermint Lounge became Manhattan's favorite party in the summer of 1961. The dingy Greenwich Village flesh spa bore scant resemblance to

The Stork Club and El Morocco uptown. Yet when New York *Journal-American* society columnist Cholly Knickerbocker (Igor Cassini) spotted a small cadre of jet setters in the club one night, he ran an item that turned the Peppermint Lounge into the city's high grade social epicenter.

To get a table you needed to spray $20 bills every which way and have a line in the *Social Register*. But street-living pre-fad customers lined the Peppermint bar and took up the dance floor, maintaining an air of seedy authenticity.

The twisting at the Peppermint was a little different from what had gone on before. There were a few variations—a tendency to dip more and find some level of synchronicity between flailing arms and twisting hips—but, at the Lounge, clothes made the manics. Society damsels showed up in wildly frilled costumes, made especially for the Peppermint floor show, that flapped and fluttered while the wearer shook.

The Peppermint gave new life to a dance craze that had already been a major hit with teenagers. The media attention made twisting legitimate for the Smart Set and everyone else. There were even reports that Jackie Kennedy twisted in the White House.

With the sensation revived, Chubby Checker's 1960 hit record made an unprecedented leap back to the top of the charts. It hit No. 1 for a two-week stretch in January 1962 and was replaced by Joey Dee and the Starlighters' recording of "Peppermint Twist," which reigned for the next three weeks.

Before the year was out there were dozens of other hot-selling Twist singles, including Elvis Presley's "Rock-a-Hula Baby," Sam Cooke's "Twistin' the Night Away," The Isley Brothers' "Twist and Shout," and "Dear Lady Twist" by Gary "U.S." Bonds.

There were also a run of twist movies during the Christmas season, 1961, led by Columbia Pictures' *Twist Around the Clock* and Paramount's *Hey Let's Twist*. Later came *Viva La Twist*, filmed in Paris with a special appearance by Joey Dee, and *Doin' the Twist* with Louis Prima. *Teenage Millionaire*, with pop singer Jimmy Clanton, Zasu Pitts, and Rocky Graziano, was given an updated opening by United Artists after the fad hit. Chubby Checker appeared briefly in the new version, and the film was advertised as a twist movie.

Twisting underwent waves of analysis and was the target of no small amount of outrage. In January 1962, a disgusted Tampa, Florida, city council banned the dance at its community center. At the dedication of his presidential library in Abilene, Kansas, Dwight Eisenhower deplored what he considered a decline in American morality and decency, and he singled out modern art and the twist for special scorn.

When the craze spread to other parts of the world in 1962, it was widely viewed as a corrupting influence from the United States. The foreign minister of South Africa complained that his country's youth had adopted "strange gods from the United States," including the Twist, rock and roll, the spirit of the beatnik, and the ducktail.

Official Moscow mocked the Twist, but it caught on with Russian youth and stood for more than a decade as the most popular modern dance in the country. Long after the dance had faded elsewhere in the world, Muscovites were still grinding out cigarette butts in their night spots.

Observers pegged the popularity of the Twist to many things, including the need to shake off societal frustrations and frolic in a manner that would be considered lewd in virtually any other context. Some academics put the Twist in a general category of craziness inspired by an angst-ridden Cold War era.

By the fall of 1962 the dance was fading fast, despite frantic Chubby Checker singles titled "Let's Twist Again" and "Don't Knock the Twist." A few adults were still at it, but kids were doing the Hully Gully, Mashed Potato, Watusi, Pony, Slop, Locomotion, and Wobble.

The new dances were kookier and more choreographic, but they all derived from the Twist; none ever surpassed it.

American Fads

THE LIMBO

The limbo, America's favorite exotic dance and party rouser in the early sixties, was actually a sacred funeral rite imported from the West Indies.

It was a dance for contortionists—the act of bending over backward and scooting underneath a crossbar while allowing only the feet to touch the ground.

If the Twist was easy to do, the Limbo was not. Clearing the underside of a low-slung pole required a slender and supple frame, and lots of practice.

Nevertheless, Americans everywhere were leaning back and enjoying the acrobatic fad. At millions of social gatherings, crowds of revelers stood around makeshift limbo pits and encouraged one another to greater depths.

The stunt drew exposure in the 1960 film *Where The Boys Are*, a classic tale of fun-seeking college students from the frozen North converging on Fort Lauderdale, Florida, during spring break. A limbo party featured briefly on the screen typified frolicsome springtime in Fort Lauderdale and helped spread the dance across the country. Meanwhile, Wham-O® Manufacturing Co. came out with the Limbo Party Game that included two posts with bases in the shapes of footprints, a crossbar, a 45-rpm calypso record and an explanation of how limboing was done.

Interest had begun to dwindle some when in 1963 Chubby Checker gave new life to the fad by following up a series of Twist records with the smash hit "Limbo Rock." The release soared to the top of the pop charts and became *Cashbox* magazine's No. 1 record for the entire year.

Checker's "how low can you go?" refrain became a national catchphrase that still occasionally rattles around in the heads of those who heard the song 300 or 400 times in early 1963.

In February, Parkway Records released Checker's album *Limbo Party*, which included the number one smash and titles like "Mary Ann Limbo," "Lala Limbo," "When The Saints Go Limbo In," and several Latin tunes meant to accompany the exotic dance. So successful was the album that just three months later, Checker came back with an album called *Let's Limbo More*.

In Trinidad, the Limbo was an ancient funeral dance. Chanting and clapping mourners took turns leaning backward and wriggling beneath a bamboo pole while grieving for the dead. By squeezing under with only the soles or sides of the feet touching, the dancers symbolized the difficult passage of the soul to final glory. Upsetting the bamboo or touching the ground was like being trapped forever in the staging area between Heaven and Hell—the place called Limbo.

As the chant grew louder and the clapping faster, the bamboo pole was set closer to the ground. An accomplished limbo artist could maneuver through a foot or less of passageway by lying parallel to the ground and creating a broad center of balance. The legs were spread far apart, and the dancer nosed beneath the stick in a completely supine position.

The renowned Trinidad dancer Boscoe Holder first recognized the artistic possibilities of the Limbo ritual and incorporated it into performances of his dance company in the late 1940's. Other dancers began using it on the island and by the mid–1950's American tourists were being entertained in nightclubs by partially clothed dancers passing beneath flaming bars. Delighted vacationers could hardly wait to try it themselves and they carried it home to friends—thereby planting the seeds of the United States craze.

Gradually, the limbo gained momentum. Teenagers did it to a rock and roll beat, beatniks limboed to bongo music, and adults tried it at slick dinner parties without musical accompaniment. They simply propped a yardstick on two chairs, took off their shoes, and had a go at it.

In Trinidad, dancers would flatten out and then skim under

the crossbar with a series of short, quick steps or hops. But most Americans would approach the stick with a few unsteady bounces and then slowly bend their heads and torsos underneath the stick.

Subteens proved best able to snake under a low-set bar. By the time "Limbo Rock" breathed new life into the fad, kids who first saw their parents try it three or four years earlier had become quite good. The existing world record was set a few years later by a fifteen-year-old girl from Toronto, Canada, who slithered under a flaming bar mounted only 6⅛ inches off the floor.

When Checker's hit record slumped, so did the Limbo sensation. It had long since faded from the adult party circuit, and kids were coming out of the early sixties dance craze period. When the Beatles arrived in early 1964, limboing was dance history.

TAPS ON SHOES

Long about the time American teenage tough guys began wearing black leather and combing their hair to excess, they also hammered steel clips onto shoe bottoms and created an aural fashion.

Clicking heels was a noisome bit of nonsense that started in the big cities during the late fifties and spanned the entire nation by the early sixties. It was an underground craze that traveled like a dirty joke. Yet it spread almost as fast as a pop song on the radio.

Cleating your shoes was a "bad fad," one that grated on parents and teachers. The silver shanks scratched school corridors, gymnasium floors, kitchen tiles, and the bathroom linoleum, and made a discourteous metallic scraping sound—an amplified defiance of parental and in loco parental reminders not to scuff while walking.

As the nation was getting its dander up about "juvenile delinquents," taps became a symbol of the new rebels without causes. Taps were a sure sign of hoodlums (or at least feigning hoodlums), along with cigarette packs rolled into sleeves, switchblades, brass knuckles, and the occasional zip gun.

Standing up on newly clipped shoes was like standing on a pair of tight cymbals. They became a walking percussion instrument, which emphasized with each step that a tough customer was in transit. The midnight sound of taps on the sidewalk and the orange specks of lit cigarettes in the dark could mean trouble in some neighborhoods.

In post-James Dean teen America, the way you carried yourself on street corners and in school lavatories was everything. Hands rested on the hip, cigarettes teetered on the lip, and combs were yanked from back pockets with the head tilted slightly forward, the free hand raised to cover the comb as though it were a harmonica. It was the motion espoused by Edd (Kookie) Byrnes on television's *77 Sunset Strip* and re-created by John Travolta and Jeff Conaway after embracing in the film version of *Grease*.

Teens also stood with the backs of the hands facing forward and fingers buried knuckle deep into the front pockets. They walked with a slow, churlish gait with toes pointed outward and a rough, steady hoofbeat of heels on pavement. Taps accented the swagger. It was the only way to walk like a man.

The sound was important. On pavement it was a low-pitched, jagged noise, while in high school hallways it was sweet and streamlined, as though pulling a sword out of a steel case.

No one is quite sure how the fad started. Some think it evolved from the tradition of urban street corner tap dancing that once flourished in places like Harlem in the same way that break dancing began.

Dance apparel has always been a touchstone for fads. In recent years, hoofers have been responsible for the preppie craze of tying sweater arms around the neck; they also begat the leotard, ballet slipper, and bodyshirt sensations. Steel clips may have also been linked to the stiletto heel craze among girls. The popular late-fifties shoes made a noise to impress the boys and were likewise unpopular with school building administrators.

But taps most likely originated from the days when manufacturers put clips on shoes as heel preservers. The half-moon-shaped metal pieces sold in three different sizes for about twenty-five, fifty, and seventy-five cents apiece. They attached to the heel, although some youngsters bought toe taps used by dancers to double the volume.

Clips were fastened on with ⅝ inch or ⅞ inch flat-headed copper rivets with a thin shaft. Holes were drilled through the taps and attached either by a local shoe repair shop or the youngster himself. They were usually worn on black, sharply pointed shoes, although some wound up on penny loafers.

Besides providing a sound effect for roughnecks, taps offered other forms of entertainment. Dancing (not tap dancing) with steel clips could sound like slashing ice skates, although it was never heard on gym floors during sock hops. One of the most popular tap tricks was to make sparks by spurring hard on concrete or kicking the side of a brick building.

By 1961 and 1962 the fad had largely spread from urban communities to schools in almost every American locale. It also filtered down to junior high students, and there are widespread remembrances of fifth and sixth grade toughs tacking steel clips onto shoes and clip-clopping to class.

But most principals, at any grade level, wouldn't stand for it. Several schools passed rules against taps on shoes, and hallway monitors would be instructed to keep an ear out. Not only would clips allegedly scratch floors; it was feared a badly applied tap, or one that extended beyond the edge of the sole, would catch on floor obtrusions and cause injury.

The most famous prohibition was in the Provincetown, Massachusetts, public school system on Cape Cod. Officials there greeted junior and senior high school students in September 1965, with a widely publicized ban on extreme apparel, focusing on steel clips, garrison belts, engineer shoes, tight clothing, and other youth trimmings.

But by 1965 taps on shoes were becoming less prominent. Never a mainstream fad, steel clips lost popularity after the Beatle-inspired longhaired look chased most of the fifties hold-over styles. The black leather look consumed only a small percentage of the national high school population by the time Mod fashion arrived in 1966 and flower child and hippie dress followed in 1967 and 1968.

But as late as 1969 a few remaining shiny-haired fifties torchbearers, usually in lower-middle-class neighborhoods, represented the last vestiges of the tap shod. They were frequently worn during the short-lived wing-tip craze among late sixties greasers.

By the new decade, steel heels were history, gone the way of rumbles and raised collars. Tough guys still strutted their stuff but the sound was turned down.

WRAPAROUND GLASSES

Bausch & Lomb

American women looked to Jackie Kennedy for fashion guidance almost from the moment she set foot in the inaugural ballroom.

Her air of windblown aristocracy was relished instead of resented. She became the transcendent trendsetter, a fashion phenomenon whose bouffant hair, back-tilted hats, alligator pumps, casual sleeveless dresses, and skinny golfing and sailing pants all became national fads.

America pressed its face to the fishbowl surrounding Jacqueline Kennedy. Her dress, her manner, her multilingual tongue, her faint voice sounding like the breathless wealth of which F. Scott Fitzgerald wrote, drew endless fascination. There was a fuss wherever she went, prompting her husband to tell the French, "I am the man who accompanied Jacqueline Kennedy to Paris."

Whatever she wore—pillbox hats, equestrian breeches, cloth coats—was endorsed for all womenkind, regardless of class or custom. But probably nothing the First Lady wore transformed public taste like the curved sun spectacles that wrapped around her head like the face-form goggles of early motorists.

Newspaper and magazine photographs of Mrs. Kennedy wearing wraparound shades touched off the unisex "Jackie glasses" craze of 1962 and helped bring sunglasses—once restricted to old ladies on beaches—into the fashion forefront. The country went clamoring for "wraparound" sunglasses, retailers were pestered for "shades like Jackie's," and manufacturers began to respond. By the fall of 1963 a record number of Americans were hiding behind them morning, noon, and very late at night.

Designers at Purdy, a Madison Avenue optician, were perhaps the originators of the wraparound look in the United States. The firm had some curved spectacles manufactured in Italy and sold two pairs to Jacqueline Kennedy.

The wide frames swept around the face from the bridge of the nose to the temples. They were striking eyewear with an almost lethal appearance, given to suggesting life not in the fast lane, but in the jet stream.

Curved glasses also had practical application, offering a panorama unhindered by peripheral lens posts or shafts of sunlight and dirt particles intruding from the wide angle. Within two years sportsmen took them hunting out of functional consideration. But the real attraction of wraparounds was their hint of monied restlessness, an appearance that made them all but standard equipment on exotic Italian sports cars.

Jackie began wearing them during the spring of 1962, and photographers were there on behalf of fashion history. As quickly as pictures were published, the country went curvature crazy. By early May, one Manhattan optician advertised "the fabulous Jackie sunglasses" in his window front. At Purdy, little more than a block away, newspaper photos of Jacqueline Kennedy wearing wraparound lenses were pasted onto a cardboard sign in the window. She was wearing the Panaram Sport Glasses designed and sold by the store.

Purdy sold two versions—one with a plastic frame for $15.00 and a rimless wraparound manufactured in France for

$17.50. Other makers followed with models ranging in price from under $2.00 for plastic lenses to more than $20.00 for a ground-glass pair sold in fine stores.

The White House took steps to halt what looked like a product endorsement by the First Lady. Presidential counsel Lee C. White notified the Better Business Bureau of Metropolitan New York that connecting Jacqueline Kennedy with the glasses violated long-standing policy against using the names or likenesses of the president and his family for commercial ventures.

The Better Business Bureau in turn warned stores against attaching the name "Jackie glasses" to wraparound styles. Retailers complied, but the many thousands of men and women who wore them throughout the summer of 1962 knew they were just like Jackie's.

The popularity of wraparounds was only the beginning of an American love affair with shades that has never ceased. By 1964, 134 million pairs of dark glasses were being sold in the United States every year, compared to 60 million in 1956.

Not all the credit belonged to Jacqueline Kennedy. Marcello Mastroianni wore sunglasses in Federico Fellini's *La Dolce Vita*, Audrey Hepburn put on round, lollipop shades in *Breakfast at Tiffany's*, and Princess Grace wore them to keep from squinting at the summer sun in Monte Carlo.

Dozens of styles have fallen in and out of favor since sunglasses became standard in America. Among them, wire-rim aviators, tortoise shells, mirror glasses, mod visor shades, and granny glasses.

Wraparounds were no longer haute couture by the fall of 1962, but they regained a national audience in 1964 after top manufacturers like Foster Grant and Bausch & Lomb brought out versions. They were part of the pre-Mod teen styles of late 1964—usually accompanying tight pants and pointed Beatle boots on both men and women.

New Wave fashion made room for a thinner wraparound look in the early eighties. They were dark, distant cousins of "Jackie glasses," but they brought back an almost surreal memory of the former First Lady and her days in the sun.

TROLL DOLLS

Photograph of Norfins®—The Second Generation of Thomas Dam Trolls; Courtesy of E.F.S. Marketing Associates, Inc., Exclusive Importer

Troll Dolls

The year was 1963 and there was magic in the air. A grinning, wild-haired imp had cast a powerful spell over hundreds of thousands of U.S. college girls and charmed his way into dormitory rooms across the country.

The spellbinder was the "troll doll," a captivating pixie that turned out to be more than a co-ed heartthrob. By early 1964, everyone from superstitious lawyers to Mrs. Lyndon B. Johnson was taken with the troll.

At first glance the doll seemed an inconsequential bubblegum machine prize, and homely at that. But trolls—also known as "Dammit Dolls," "Dam Things," "Wish Niks," or "Drolls"—were more than met the eye. They were said to possess a touch of elfin enchantment, which helped them become the most popular good luck charm since the rabbit's foot.

The unshakable belief among many owners was that the statuette looked after them. As such, troll dolls were carted around in pocketbooks and pockets and taken out frequently for a little trendy show and tell.

The miniature fairyfolk proved the appeal of funny-looking figurines exactly twenty years before the Cabbage Patch Kids. Just like the adorably dough-faced Cabbage crop, the uncomely trolls proved irresistible.

Troll dolls ranged from three inches to roughly a foot tall. Most had a shock of white sheep's wool hair that swept upward several inches. The basic troll was bereft of clothes, paunchy and glassy-eyed, with nostrils that flared across its tiny face and ears which stuck out like jug handles. The final touch was an endearing U-shaped grin that helped make trolls the last word in cute.

According to legend, a poor Danish woodcutter named Thomas Dam carved the first troll doll as a birthday gift for his teenage daughter because he could afford no other present. The doll he cut from wood was based on the mythic creatures of Scandinavian folklore, which are as old as time and invisible to all but children and kindhearted adults.

They were known as pranksters and merrymakers who lived in caves beneath the Nordic mountains, forever eluding humankind. If caught, the supernatural creatures were thought to lavish luck and prosperity on their captors. For Dam, who supposedly carved his mannequin in the late 1950's, the troll did just that.

As the story goes, his daughter was entranced by the gift and showed it to friends in their Danish village. A toy shop owner noticed the doll and the rest was hysteria. Dam was soon arranging for the manufacture of his item, and a few years later he brought it to the United States. "Dammit Dolls" were an immediate hit in this country. The trolls became the second best-selling doll of the entire decade—behind Barbie.

They caught on first with college girls—replacing stuffed animals as their foremost object of inanimate affection. They were so devilishly cute that owners imbued them with irrepressible, sometimes mischievous personalities, and magical powers imported from the Scandinavian countryside.

The good luck dolls were standard accompaniment for midterm and final examinations in the fall of 1963. They lorded over dormitory rooms from the tops of dressers, looking down with an ever-present grin and a glow of good fortune.

With mounting publicity for the kooky new campus rage, trolls found a wider acceptance. By early 1964, high school sports teams took them as mascots, small children began to covet them, and many adults bought and believed in the trolls. A St. Louis attorney credited a doll with boosting the size of his practice, while aviatrix Betty Miller had a troll as her copilot when, in late 1963, she duplicated Amelia Earhart's 7,400-mile flight of 1935.

The popularity of his dolls led Dam to market them in various sizes, ranging in price from $1.95 for baby versions to $5.95 for an adult troll. The later dolls could be outfitted with different hair or costumes and augmented with a selection of props that included a miniature ironing board, dishes, a motorcycle, and a Troll Bank with vertical slots in the back. The U.S. manufacturer of Dammit Dolls, Royalty Design of Florida, based in Hialeah, also produced elephants, giraffes, lions, cows, horses, and donkeys to round out its collection of trolls.

Uneeda Doll Company, another prominent troll maker, produced an identical figurine called Wish Nik. Uneeda's troll had a major stake in the 1963–64 craze, and the company produced several versions of the basic doll.

The fad cooled when school let out in June 1964, but trolls remain collectibles today. One collector is Go-Gos', lead singer Brenda Carlisle, who has her dolls outfitted in miniature punk garb.

"I'm sure they got the idea for E.T. from Dammit Dolls," said Carlisle during a 1985 interview on the Cinemax cable channel program *Album Flash*. She then picked up a troll and cooed, "Ohhhh, you're so cute."

A second generation of Thomas Dam trolls, called Nortins,® are now sold in America. They are imported by E.F.S. Marketing of Farmingdale, New York.

Authentic Dammit Dolls, bearing Thomas Dam's mark on the back, are said to be the most valued. Some fetch as much as $75 among collectors. One-time fanatics who kept their dolls benefited from their enduring enthusiasm for troll mythology. The storied characters, ever growing in value, are still bestowing good fortune.

GO-GO BOOTS

Photograph by Harold M. Lambert

Go-Go Boots

69

Boots were part of the package when the miniskirt came over from Paris in early 1965. As *Newsweek* said of the new thigh-high hemlines, "The adjustment will have to be more than psychological. Only low-heeled shoes or boots set off a short-skirted figure properly."

Indeed, bootwear was soon basic to women's fashion; the first on the scene were the calf-level "à go-gos," a broad-heeled, bright white leather or virgin vinyl style that became all but mandatory for discotheque dancing.

The new "short, short skirt," accompanied always by boots and patterned stockings, turned up in the hottest spots on both coasts—the fledgling discotheques of Manhattan and Los Angeles and the coffeehouses in Boston and San Francisco.

They were worn first by a fashion avant-garde made up of vogueish teens and co-eds, but they became a rage for all ages. Little girls went gaga over the big girl look, while adults liked their kicky kid stuff appeal and the way go-gos helped them wear short skirts more gracefully.

By 1966 and the onset of Mod finery from London's Carnaby Street, go-gos were very soon gone—replaced by chunky-heel shoes and higher boots. But they remain the most memorable feminine footgear of the sixties, a style that reflected both the new exuberance in women's fashion and an unsurpassed era in American nightclubbing.

André Courrèges was the Parisian most responsible. In February 1965, he introduced white dresses that hung three inches above the knee and white mid-calf boots, known in fashion circles as "kid boots." The sensation overshadowed simultaneous collections from Coco Chanel and other established French fashion designers. Courrèges's radical vision was reviled by colleagues, but there was no stopping short skirts. They were on the next jet to New York, and the designer was adamant that the boots go too. "Without them," he said, "short skirts look ridiculous."

It was in the choicest discotheques that the boots made their reputation and took their name. On January 15, 1964, a Los Angeles nightclub called Whiskey à Go-Go opened on Sunset Strip and by early 1965 was proclaimed "the hottest club in America" by *Esquire* magazine. The likes of Johnny Rivers performed live, but the club was equipped with a huge stereo system and the emphasis was on recorded music and pure exultant dancing.

Music at the Whiskey was controlled by dancers in a large, glass-walled room that hovered over the floor. They spun records and shimmied in white, wonderful boots and short frilly dresses that flapped when they moved.

Go-go girls are an enduring image of the era. They were untouchable discotheque dolls who often danced in giant, ornate birdcages—an idea borrowed from the French. They would frug, swim, jerk, and sometimes entertain the patrons by demonstrating new dances. In lesser clubs they were viewed as bump and grinders, but in places like the Whiskey they were stars.

Almost all go-go girls wore go-go boots, including the perky dancers on NBC's prime time pop music program *Hullabaloo* in the summer of 1965. Suddenly, girls all over the country were clamoring for white boots à go-go.

What had started as an accessory to short skirts had developed a fashion life of its own. The boots flourished through the remainder of 1965 and peaked in popularity during the early months of 1966 as dozens of manufacturers took them to market.

Some were furred or fringed from the top. A few were black-and-white and others straight black. They looked like loose-fitting rubber overshoes that were apt to fly off while you were dancing. Some fashion observers regarded them as a female version of black Beatle boots, which had a similar heel, but a more sharply pointed toe.

Queen of the go-gos was singer Nancy Sinatra. She was linked to the fad in 1966 when "These Boots Are Made for Walkin'," her growling anthem that seemed to anticipate feminism, climbed the pop music charts. The record sold nearly four million copies and Nancy went on tour with two hundred and fifty pairs of boots in tow.

Her influence on young girls was enormous. In May 1985,

singing star Madonna told *Spin* magazine, "My first pop idol was Nancy Sinatra. Go-go boots, miniskirt, fake eyelashes—she was cool."

Go-go boots did as they were asked—balancing the new mini look and buying time for short skirts in combination with other footwear. They helped adjust the eye to the new American hemline.

But by spring 1966, go-gos were drowning in a sea of Mod. During the red-hot discotheque summer of 1966, when clubs like The Cheetah and Arthur in New York, Le Bison in Chicago, and The Trips in Los Angeles gained fame, the short white "kid boots" were nowhere to be seen. Hemlines were going even higher, but the companion boots had fallen by the wayside.

In 1967, high-rise foot fashion appeared. Thigh-, knee-, and hip-length boots served as a transition between Mod styles and flower child garb. But go-gos, late of teenybopper fame, were the antithesis of hippie sensibilities.

They reflected times and places which were hopelessly outdated. The beat went on, but go-go boots came off.

SKATEBOARDS

Kevin J. Thatcher, Courtesy of *Thrasher* Magazine

One of the great makeshift toys of urban America was made by tacking roller skate wheels onto short slabs of wood that carted standing riders down steep inclines.

It had been around for decades when resourceful California youngsters in the early sixties began making improvements in the ancient plaything that touched off a local craze. Soon manufacturers were turning out relatively sophisticated models, the name "skateboard" took hold, and by 1965, kids all over the country were engaged—perilously—in the sport of sidewalk surfing.

Skateboards made for an inland version of the California beach surfing craze, giving young landlubbers a chance to mimic the oceangoing moves of their coastal brethren.

After a summer or two of broken bones, most kids got off boards for good. But twelve years later, skateboards came careening back stronger than ever.

Aficionados built a better board, enhanced its maneuverability, and at the same time removed some of the risk. What had been an ungovernable skate for daredevils only was transformed into a hard-tracking sport vehicle. Lavish parks were erected with high-bank curves and obstacle courses, serious competition was inaugurated, and there was even talk of putting skateboards in the Olympic Games.

While tinkering with the old, inflexible rollerboard rigs, California boys in the early sixties mounted two-foot pieces of wood or plastic on wheels in a way that allowed the riding surface to dip from side to side with the shifting of weight—like a real surfboard. Unlike the original urban toys with their rigid topsides, the new boards could change direction.

In the fall of 1963 commercial versions appeared in southern California under such names as Surf Skater, Makaha, and Bun Buster. Local sales reached the fifty-thousand mark within a few months, and makers began targeting a broader market.

By early 1965, kids everywhere were shooting the curl on plastic and wooden boards priced from $1.98 to $50 for a motorized model. Manufacturers sold $30 million worth in 1965 and never looked back.

Adults usually stayed away from skateboards after one or two falls. But kids rode them with a vengeance and some even mastered a few tricks. They did miraculous riding handstands, raced downhill while reclining feet first on their backs, and jumped over hurdles off a rolling board.

The problem was hard clay wheels that tracked poorly and couldn't absorb so much as a pebble without bucking the rider. A smoother, more controllable ride was possible with composition wheels made of plastic, paper, and finely ground walnut shells. But the soft wheels wore out quickly, sometimes after a few hours of hard use.

There were only halfhearted attempts to turn skateboarding

into a competitive sport in the sixties. Students at Williams, Amherst, and Wesleyan assembled for what they called the first intercollegiate skateboard championship at the Middletown, Connecticut, campus of Wesleyan in May 1965. Competitors demonstrated trick-riding by standing atop wastebaskets perched on rolling boards and slithered through obstacle courses staked out with beer cans. First place went to Williams, but there was no second annual championship at which to defend the title.

Only authorities took skateboarding seriously in the sixties. After several children were injured rolling into traffic, cities in New Jersey, Massachusetts, New York, and California banned them on all public thoroughfares. Hospitals across the country reported numerous accidents suffered while skateboarding, and that didn't count the bumps, bruises, and scrapes treated at home.

But it was neither official reproach nor frequent injuries which finally prompted kids to curb their skateboards. The trouble was that skateboards could never really be piloted; you simply hung on with your toes. As a result, the toy never got much beyond the stage of novelty

But a breakthrough came in 1973, long after most skateboards had been closeted and forgotten about. A southern Californian named Frank Nasworthy invented a urethane wheel that held tight corners, enabling riders to make sharp angle turns and quick pivots and even zip up the sides of high embankments while letting the centrifugal force be with them.

Next came more advanced axle assemblies and light and lithe fiberglass bodies. By late 1976 manufacturers were producing exotic, elaborate, and expensive boards, and a new breed of youthful enthusiasts bought them as sporting goods, not toys. Some spent up to $200 for separate deck and wheels and assembled the unit themselves. They also purchased helmets, knee and elbow pads, wrist guards, and gloves, hiking annual sales of skateboard paraphernalia to almost half a billion dollars in 1978.

The new riders—mostly under age fifteen—performed eye-popping maneuvers which made even the best sixties skateboarders look crude by comparison. To hone their skills they took to empty swimming pools, expressway culverts—any place with near vertical walls that could be climbed at high speed.

Of course, some of the old headaches had not gone away. The Consumer Product Safety Commission warned, in 1977, of injuries to skateboarders, with or without protective gear. In some areas, fanatics feuded with bicyclists for occupancy of public right-of-way. In New York City, skateboard riders petitioned the Department of Parks and Recreation for a lane to themselves in Central Park, while bicyclists tried to get them banned from the park.

Into the void came such vast skateboard stadia as the three-and-a-half acre Skateworld near Los Angeles. Skilled riders swept through concrete bobsled runs at breakneck speed and executed acrobatic stunts with names like "flip kicks," "end overs," "Gorilla jumps," and "one-wheel peripheral commitment."

The new interest spawned sanctioned competitions. Skateboarding was all the way back, and even after the mania began to fade in the eighties, there remained a devoted core of young hellcats who rode on.

IRONING HAIR

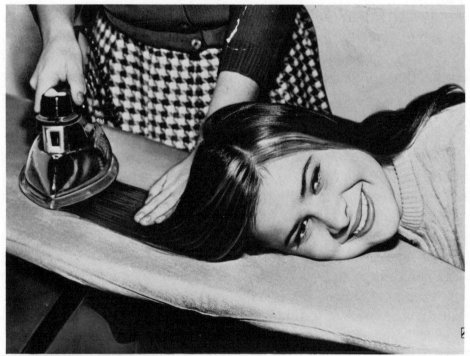

AP/Wide World Photos

In early 1965, young American women came out from under their curlers, stoked up clothing irons to "silk" and "wash and wear" and made with the ultimate heat treatment.

Girls who had attended to bouffant extravaganzas for years suddenly stopped sleeping on rollers and went straight. Across the country, tease combs were put aside and hair problems literally were ironed out.

Naturally curly tresses, once prized and pampered, were

stretched out on ironing boards and put into place. Young women who had been making waves with curling irons turned to an uncurling iron to make them disappear.

There were lots of discouraging words in 1965. Several hair specialists warned that direct application of intense heat could permanently damage hair. Some adults were disturbed that young women went to such radical lengths to alter their appearance. A few felt it showed just how dangerously extreme young people could be in an effort to shock elders and bend to peer pressure.

At first, ironing hair was no more than a quick and easy way to bring down your overhead. With long and straight in style, girls with curls could either pay $25 for an anti-permanent or apply an odorous, altogether unpleasant home straightener. The solution was to plug in an electric iron and do the job in a matter of minutes with no fuss or muss.

But what started as a cheap shortcut to fashionable hair became a fad itself. Yielding to the ironing board became a rite of passage not unlike the ear-piercing craze of a half-decade earlier. Everyone was heating their hair; girls with naturally straight hair periodically used an iron to make it even straighter.

The revolutionary new hairstyle is believed to have begun with singer Joan Baez, then at the height of her popularity. The folk singer reportedly kept her hair straight to escape the tedium of femininity. In so doing, she helped launch a trend among young women that would last through the remainder of the decade. Whether long, short, or somewhere in-between, there was little interest in lavish curls again until well into the 1970's.

Long and straight was also the message American girls were getting from Britain, then a hotbed of popular music. English singers like Marianne Faithful and Dusty Springfield and Beatle Paul McCartney's girlfriend, Jane Asher, kept it flowing and curl-free, with bangs hanging over the eyes.

Models on television and in fashion advertising were also wearing a sheepdog look in early 1965, further influencing young women to get rid of waves, frizz, ringlets, and other entanglements.

The hot iron fad started in Boston boarding schools, where Baez, having started out singing in the small clubs of Cambridge, was a heroine. By April 1965, young women everywhere were submitting to the power of the press.

The dramatic change in appearance was part of the fun. So accustomed were American males to teased and billowy hair that long and straight proved shocking. College co-eds in the spring of 1965 stunned a nation of fathers and boyfriends with the new hairdos. "My father almost fainted when he saw me in the straight hair look," said a sophomore from Colorado Women's College that spring.

Through 1965, girls continued to apply the heat—finding they needed to return to the ironing board after each washing to keep matters straight. The procedure was relatively simple. The girl being treated sat eye-level to the board and extended her hair across the ironing surface. A friend went over an inch at a time, taking about ten minutes to complete the job.

Some girls claimed that ironing not only straightened hair, but made it fine and soft. But there was growing fear about the hazards of overdoing it, or using an iron that was too hot.

While the hairstyle survived, irons were out by mid-1966. Some of the heat was off when Dr. Robert Berger, a New York University dermatologist, reported that ironing "may cause so much breakage that the hair will look thin in places." The story of a University of Wisconsin student who accidentally burned the shape of an iron into her roommate's hair also helped kill the thrill.

Beauticians today say all the fuss about harming hair with an iron was overblown, since curling irons work in the same way as clothing irons. But ill-advised or not, ironing hair was becoming outmoded. Even if the hair was fine, the novelty had worn thin.

Ben Martin

American Fads
80

SUPER BALL®

Wham-O® Manufacturing Co., the miracle-working maker of the Hula Hoop® and Frisbee® disc, bounced back into the news in 1965 with an explosive knob of rubber called Super Ball.®

Dropped from shoulder level, a high potency Super Ball® snapped nearly all the way back; thrown down, it could leap over a three-story building; flung into a wall with spin, it kicked back with remarkable reverse English.

The supercharged sphere, about the size and color of a plum, was America's most popular plaything in the summer and fall of 1965. By Christmas, just six months after it was introduced by Wham-O,® seven million balls had sold at ninety-eight cents apiece.

Proud father of the bouncing baby ball was a California chemist named Norman Stingley. In his spare time, he compressed a synthetic rubber material under 3,500 pounds of pressure per square inch and created a ball with unprecedented resilience.

Stingley offered it to his employer, Bettis Rubber Company, of Whittier, California, but was turned down. Since the rubber hardpack tended to fall apart quickly, it was feared the product would never be marketable.

But Wham-O,® a company with a reputation for taking brilliant ideas off the street (the Frisbee® was freelanced to the firm by a carpenter), agreed to work with Stingley on his idea. For several months they sought a more durable substance and finally concocted a ball that stood up under normal use, although it still lost large chunks when smashed against rough surfaces.

With imperfections whittled away, the Super Ball® was bound for glory, a sensation waiting to happen. An old hand at marketing crazes, Wham-O® gave the bulletized balls a big promotional send-off and they caught on right away. Adolescent boys and girls discovered them first, but grown-ups were soon buying them, too.

Uses were many and varied. Super Balls® were bounced over rooftops, dribbled by skateboarders, ricocheted among adjoining surfaces and used for Superballing the Jacks. The tightly compacted, high friction ball could also be spun into a wall in such a way that it would bounce back at the barrier repeatedly. Accomplished Super Ballplayers could make the self-perpetuating rubber missile hammer itself into a wall four or five times. Long lobbing covered entire city blocks, as the balls ate up the distance with kangaroo-like bounds and seemed to gather momentum as they skipped along the street. Kids also took up baseball bats and entertained Ruthian fantasies by hitting suborbital shots.

Juvenile games were inventive, but adults thought up ways of using Super Balls,® too. At the workplace they were vaulted over rows of office desktops, sent hopping down corridors, and dropped onto sidewalks and parking lots from windows several stories high. Competitors tried depositing them into far-off wastebaskets with one strategic bounce.

Presidential aide McGeorge Bundy had five dozen shipped to the White House for the amusement of staffers. At the Pacific Coast Stock Exchange, traders relieved tension by propelling them across the floor.

Super Balls® encouraged wholesome, boyish, childhood-revisited kind of fun. The only thing to fear was the sphere itself. The ball was so resilient and picked up so much reverse spin that it didn't catch easily. After slamming one into a wall you might have to duck or be struck. Black eyes and welts, about the circumference of a Super Ball,® were common to the fad, but were not enough to dampen enthusiasm.

Wham-O's® oft-repeated claim was that the ball had 92 percent resiliency—about three times that of a tennis ball—and would bounce on for about a minute after being dropped from a short distance.

The synthetic used to make the ball spring eternal was dubbed Zectron by Stingley, and there were rumors that it was made from an exotic fruit grown by crossing an East Indian rubber plant with an Outer Mongolian plumb tree. A likable, if unlikely story; when Stingley's patent was issued in March 1966, it revealed a less colorful formula. The primary element was polybutadiene, with smaller amounts of sulfur to reinforce the material and serve as a vulcanizing agent. According to the patent, the ball was molded under some one thousand pounds of pressure per square inch at a temperature of about 320 degrees Fahrenheit.

The balls were also red hot in the marketplace and pressure from retailers was intense. Output at Wham-O's® San Gabriel, California, plant and four other factories contracted to turn them out grew to one hundred seventy thousand a day by mid-November.

The appeal lasted well into 1966, although adults and kids eventually let loose of the fad. Meanwhile, there were few original Super Balls® left for posterity since most were eventually chipped into oblivion.

Yet no one who ever owned a Super Ball® has forgotten the greatest bouncer of all time. No ball in history ever behaved like the Super Ball® and none ever sold like it.

Tickner/Dickson Management

American Fads

84

GRANNY GLASSES

During the mid-sixties, when most teen music and fashion was being imported from Britain, granny glasses were an authentic American fad.

The eccentric half-frames adopted by U.S. teenagers in 1965 and 1966 were part of the Mod scene that originated in London. Yet the specs craze started halfway around the globe from Carnaby Street.

California kids began wearing pince-nez in the summer of 1965, and the trend didn't reach England until a year later. John Lennon, a Britisher and, at the time, a dedicated follower of fashion, wore a pair of grannies for the back cover photo of the Beatles' *Revolver* album, released in August 1966.

But regardless of national origin, grannies (or Ben Franklin specs, as they were just as well known) became the most popular eyeglass frames in the country. Young people were suddenly demanding them both for prescription lenses and dark glasses.

Sunshades had been flourishing since the early sixties, but primarily among adults. They did not catch on with pop music-makers and their young fans until The Byrds began making waves up and down the California coast in 1965.

The Byrds was a pioneering combo which brought together elements of electric rock and folk lyricism. The group appealed both to Bohemians settled on the West Coast—the street people who had dubbed themselves "hippies"—and the teen set just coming down from the Beatle high of 1964.

The band had developed a big following in California clubs in the summer of 1965 when it struck with a smash hit electric version of Bob Dylan's "Mr. Tambourine Man." The Byrds were suddenly the biggest new act in American music, and everyone in the rock firmament made pilgrimages to Ciro's in Hollywood to see them perform.

There was a strange and exotic quality about the group that began with its acknowledged leader, guitarist and singer Jim McGuinn. He hunched over the microphone in the manner of Lennon, sang out the side of his mouth, and peered over the top of tiny, rectangular-shaped dark spectacles.

It turned out he wore them to protect his eyes from the stage lights, but when kids began showing up at Byrds performances with "granny glasses," it was clear he had started something.

The glasses became a trademark of McGuinn and the band, and he was soon wearing them offstage as well. The memorable fish-eye lens photograph on the cover of the *Mr. Tambourine Man* album, released in August 1965, showed McGuinn in the middle of the quintet, looking down at the camera through his Franklin frames.

When the Byrds sang their hit on network television programs like *The Ed Sullivan Show* and *Hullabaloo*, the glasses got national exposure. McGuinn also wore them for the cover photo on the band's second album, *Turn, Turn, Turn*, released in February 1966, and in March, *Newsweek* ran a prominent photo of a young girl in granny glasses to go with an extensive essay on emerging teen culture.

Manufacturers helped spread the fad with their advertising campaigns. A young Cindy Williams, who later starred on television's *LaVerne & Shirley*, wore granny glasses in a famous print ad for Foster Grant.

They were the official eyewear for American youth and like much of the Mod dress that took hold in 1966, they were a unisex trend. It was especially funky for young couples to wear matching pairs as a metaphor of romantic and sexual union.

The foundation of the fad? McGuinn started it, of course, but some observers theorized about a broader "elderly look" fascination among the young. The bifocals invented by Ben Franklin two hundred years earlier and worn by generations of grandmothers were said to be a symbol of age in contrast with vibrant youth. That helped explain the simultaneous popularity of "granny dresses," the nostalgic ankle-length frontier garb worn by young girls and banned at many schools because they were supposedly unsafe on stairs.

McGuinn was the first major pop star since Roy Orbison to wear sunglasses, but he touched off a trend among rockers and their followers. Dylan was soon hiding behind them, Brian Jones of The Rolling Stones owned several pairs, including grannies, and the Beatles wore dark glasses while videotaping performances of their new single releases in 1966. All four put on shades for the *Revolver* album jacket, although only Lennon wore McGuinn's Franklin frames.

The Mod fashion industry tried other sunglasses during 1966. Pop Art and Op Art styles came with oversized octagon, square, and rectangle frames, and lenses with stripes, checks, and one-way mirrors.

There were even full-face visors for women that looked like welders' shields. Though none of the outlandish Mod glasses were as universally popular as Ben Franklin frames, they seemed to attract more media attention.

Most of the Mod-era glasses, including the grannies, vanished by 1967. But photographs of early hippie events in California—the be-ins and love-ins and what-not—depict an occasional half-frame in the crowd. A few could even be spotted at the Monterey International Pop Music Festival in the summer of 1967.

The Byrds, meanwhile, were hurtling toward break-up. Their popularity had waned by late 1967 when the group's fifth album, *The Byrds' Greatest Hits,* was released. Dave Swaney was already observing, nostalgically, in the liner notes, "McGuinn made someone a lot of money by wearing those funny-looking Ben Franklin glasses."

Within a couple of years, McGuinn would be the only original member left in the faltering band. He was passé, and so were the glasses. Pop history, however, has been kind to both—judging one a great artist of the sixties and the other a great artifact.

SLOT CARS

Auto World, Scranton, Pennsylvania

The steady buzz of motorized slot cars on a tabletop track was the sound effect of the sixties for millions of American kids.

Fifteen years before the video game explosion, youngsters got a similar kick at the "wheel" of zippy plastic cars which traveled up to six hundred miles per hour at scale.

The slot car fad gave rise to thousands of racing emporiums throughout the country. Multilevel, labyrinthine speedways extending several yards long drew enthusiasts day and night at the height of the craze in 1965. It also caught on with adults, many of whose attention to detail surpassed even that of model railroaders.

The industry zoomed past $150 million in sales that year, more than Americans spent on surfing, skiing, and golf. Some felt it would eventually bypass bowling in the realm of family entertainment. It did not. Slot car racing was finally exposed as a short-lived fad, but it has never vanished completely.

Cars guided by small fins under the nose, which were inserted into grooves in the track, scooted around tracks of four to eight lanes. Electrical power surged into the vehicles via underside brushes which made contact with metal strips. The strength of the electric current determined the speed of the race car and could be controlled by a rheostat in the hands of the "driver." Wheeling a slot car through a series of twists and turns required skill. Too much speed while cornering would send a car spinning violently out of control.

The plastic models were replicas of real automobiles produced in scales ranging from $1/87$ to $1/24$. Most were bought preassembled at prices ranging from under $3 for a stripped-down Corvette Sting Ray to $8 for a well-appointed Maserati 5000.

Some hobbyists purchased raw materials and built their own cars from scratch—tinkering with the small electric motors and miniature bodies and frames to achieve maximum speed.

Popular ploys included lightening a chassis by drilling holes, treating tire rubber to improve traction, and upgrading engine performance by rewinding the tiny coils. Amateur car builders could work with almost twenty varieties of rubber, hundreds of body shells, and innumerable styles.

Tabletop racing buffs traced slot cars to Britain near the turn of the century. The first cars were big, expensive and slow. However, the invention of alnico (a magnetically-charged alloy of aluminum-nickel-cobalt), in the early 1930's, enabled the small motors to turn up to twenty-five thousand revolutions per minute. Within a few years, lighter plastic models became available, and advances in the art of miniaturization pushed cars to breathtaking speeds.

Slot car racing had a small, but loyal following in England for several years, although the high price of cars limited its popularity. Even while American kids were buying cars with allowance money, British youngsters were paying up to $50 for a respectable model.

Tabletop racing kits arrived in the United States in 1959, when Aurora Plastics Corp. introduced $20–$50 Model Motoring sets consisting of two-inch cars on HO-scale track. Commercial raceways began turning up in hobby shops two years later and the pastime picked up momentum until it reached $100 million in sales in 1963—overtaking electric trains.

In early 1965, slot car racing exploded. An estimated 3.5 million persons, mostly adolescents, were running cars on a regular basis. Over five thousand racing organizations were formed in the United States and magazines with titles like *Model Car Science* and *Model Car and Truck* served up a steady diet of news and information for buffs.

Racing centers dotted every area of the country, including three hundred in California alone. Some slot shops featured tracks up to two hundred twenty feet long, with winding figure-eights and over-and-under designs. Verisimilitude was painstaking at many tracks. Courses were often accented with elaborate Lilliputian scenery, including landscaping, detailed pit areas, and bleachers with tiny spectators. Racers could buy an hour's track time for about $1.50 and rent a car for another half dollar if they didn't have their own.

For serious hobbyists there was plenty of sanctioned competition. In the San Francisco area, nine tournaments were held every weekend in the summer of 1965. Races sponsored that year by the International Model Racing Society carried $28,000 in prize money, and the American Model Car Raceways, Incorporated put up $100,000 in awards for a series of team events.

Racing squads formed at Princeton, Yale, UCLA, Penn State, and other universities. Competitors flocked to meets with vast and valuable equipment stockpiles.

The slot car fad was also played out in countless cellars and living rooms across the country. Small 1/87 scale sets could be purchased for as little as $20, while some fanatics spent up to $1,500 outfitting their homes with long and lavish track layouts.

Through special arrangements, slot car companies brought out scale versions of new automobiles at the same time they were introduced by major auto manufacturers. After the real Ford Mustang was unveiled in the spring of 1964, Aurora's plastic version quickly became the most popular slot car of all time—selling about a million models in 1965.

Meanwhile, dozens of celebrities admitted to being slot car owners and operators, including Walter Cronkite, Mel Torme, and real-life race driver Dan Gurney. Attorney General Robert Kennedy drew attention to the fad by racing a model car on a slot track during the June dedication of John F. Kennedy Park in Washington, D.C.

Slot cars were hot cars again in 1966, but slumped the next year as track rentals and sales of models and accessories fell off. Many hobby shops which installed enormous tracks costing up to $8,000 were dismantling them by the dawn of the new decade.

The sport was eclipsed by other amusements, but lots of tinkering and racing still goes on. Many model car speed freaks, initiated during the mid-sixties slot car furor which swept the nation, have never eased off the throttle.

American Fads

SIXTIES BUTTON CRAZE

It was the fall of 1967 at Tompkins Square Park in New York and the moment was special. The legendary San Francisco rock group Country Joe and the Fish had come east for the first time to play for the Greenwich Village hippies, and they were being warmly received.

The good vibrations were almost audible. Then, in the midst of bicoastal communing, someone tossed a carton of lapel buttons in the air, mostly reading "Pray for Sex." Dozens of young people picked them up and pinned them on their chests. It was a sign of the times.

Next to passing marijuana cigarettes, passing buttons was the great goodwill gesture of the late sixties counterculture. The mores-shattering generation delighted in the button media. Many were obscene, but they were also humorous, serious, political, apolitical, ribald, witty, literary, intellectual, anti-intellectual, religious, sacrilegious, left-wing, right-wing, and middle of the road. They said anything and everything, and young people pinned them on their chests to get something off their chests.

But what started as personal billboarding among kids spread to society at large. Buttons were suddenly celebrating all there was to celebrate, even commercial products. The new reliance on lapelese to get points across reached final form in 1975, when President Gerald Ford sought—disastrously—to curry support for his "Whip Inflation Now" program by having hundreds of thousands of WIN buttons manufactured.

In the early 1960's the bumper sticker emerged as a popular new form of expression. Suddenly, the widest possible assortment of messages began to crop up on the rear guards of automobiles. It was first reported on a car fender that "Mary Poppins Is a Junkie" and "Apple Pie Is Fluoridated."

The joy of startling complete strangers that began with bumper stickers, infected the sixties youth movement. But since few owned automobiles, buttoning up was the best way to express social and political cynicism and also to bear witness to lack of inhibitions. Part of the fun was watching polite society jaws drop and bluenoses turn red with anger at a permissive missive on your shirt.

The button binge was everywhere by early 1967. The craze started almost simultaneously in the Haight-Ashbury section of San Francisco and in Greenwich Village, and later spread to all points in-between. One could find hundreds of hippie bromides on buttons at underground emporiums across the country. Anything to fit your mood or manner could be acquired for spare change.

Among the first and most famous adages were "America Has Gone to Pot," "Tune In, Turn On, Drop Out," "If It Feels Good, Do It," and "Make Love, Not War." All endured as epigrams of the era.

Next came humor ("Save Water, Shower with a Friend," and "Defoliate Forest Lawn") followed by racy directives ("If It Moves, Fondle It" and "Be Creative: Invent a Sexual Perversion").

Button sloganeers seemed to derive their inspiration from graffiti writers. For example, "Socrates Eats Hemlock." Lapel literature employed the same sort of pith and punmanship which adorned the walls of public bathrooms for decades.

The buttons railed against the war in Vietnam ("Draft Beer, Not Boys," "Burn Pot, Not People"), tweaked conservatives ("Reduce Reagan 10 Per Cent," "J. Edgar Hoover Sleeps with a Nightlight"), and urged broadmindedness on issues like homosexuality ("Love Is a Many-Gendered Thing").

Readers were exhorted to "Go Naked," "Kill a Commie for Christ," "Cure Virginity," and "Hire the Morally Handicapped." In take-offs on the "God Is Dead" theme, they pronounced that "God Is a Teenybopper," "God Is Alive in the White House," "God Is Alive and Well and Living in Mexico," and "God Is a 5,000—foot Jelly Bean."

Some of the buttons were blue. New York police went after

Greenwich Village button entrepreneur Mark Sloane for allegedly selling obscene buttons at his "Big Store." Sloane got into trouble when a high school principal in Matawan, New Jersey, spotted a student wearing an obscene button purchased from the Big Store. He complained to the merchant and later brought criminal charges, alleging that Sloane was offending public decency.

Sloane was arrested in December 1966, after an undercover officer bought for $1.25 five buttons he considered obscene. One read "Pornography Is Fun," another, "Lay Don't Slay." The rest were more explicit. The district attorney's office argued that the buttons were dirty, while Sloane's American Civil Liberties Union counsel said "evil is only in the mind of the beholder."

If anything, publicity over the Greenwich Village case boosted button sales in New York and elsewhere. By spring, manufacturers could not make enough to keep up with demand, and retailers could not keep them in stock. Underground Uplift in New York, one of the largest distributors of buttons, was shipping two hundred thousand a month to all parts of the country. Sloane, who stocked over two hundred fifty slogans, was selling between one hundred fifty thousand and two hundred thousand a month at home and abroad.

Controversy continued. Buttons were banned at a high school in Los Angeles in early 1967 until a wise-guy student wore one reading "God Bless America" to class and got the prohibition lifted.

Conservative backlash to hippie mottoes began to turn up on buttons. "Support Your Local Police," and "America: Love It or Leave It"—bumper sticker favorites—made the leap to lapels.

Others also recognized the power of the medium. Corporations began using buttons as important parts of advertising and promotional campaigns. The most famous was Avis Corporation's ubiquitous red "We Try Harder" button—seventy million of which were given out in twenty-three languages.

Everyone was relying on buttons and the practice continued until Ford's fiasco. The red WIN buttons seemed to mark the end of a communication era, collecting dust in a government warehouse at a much-discussed financial cost to taxpayers and immeasurable political cost to the president.

The original hippie button boom had died out several years

before. Once there were hundreds of social jabs and rejoinders to choose from, but by 1970 head shops handled only a few standard cliché pins and lots of rock band badges. The creative new personal message board of the seventies was the T-shirt. The funny upheaval buttons of the sixties were on their way to becoming collectors' items.

NEHRU
JACKETS

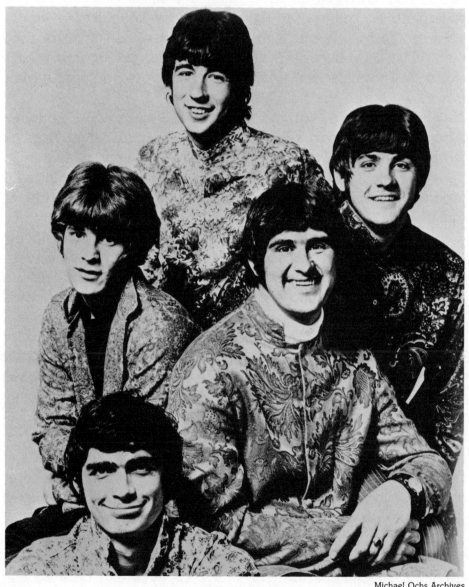

Michael Ochs Archives

Nehru Jackets

97

The Nehru jacket, worn over a turtleneck sweater with a peace medallion or love beads hanging from the neck, was one of the great uniforms of the sixties.

It started as antiwar attire, but by the spring of 1968 the Nehru had emerged as more than a political or even fashion statement. So many gray flannel refugees bought them that it became the hula hoop of American sportswear—an exotic fad that, while short-lived, paved the way for a revolution in men's clothing. It was the first of the flash that would dominate male formal wear into the next decade.

The exact origin of the craze is still debated. Entertainer Sammy Davis, Jr., says it all began in the mid-sixties when he wore a white linen Indian jacket purchased in London to a posh party in Paris. Others have credited designer Pierre Cardin, who reportedly fashioned a Nehru-style jacket following a trip to India.

But the Nehru seems to have gathered momentum in the United States as a coat for the clothes-conscientious-objector. Rock musicians wore them in concert at the Fillmore Auditorium in the fall of 1967, and thousands of others donned them as declarations of love, peace, and impeccable tailoring.

Sensing a fashion turning point, manufacturers geared up for spring introduction of the avant-garde high-collar tunics with buttons down one side and no lapels. Given a big promotional send-off, Nehrus spread from pacifists to a new set—the young, rich, and exuberant.

With the Love Generation showing signs of commercial clout, the garment industry acted fast. Nehrus in a variety of colors and fabrics were rushed into production and by spring were a common sight in major cities throughout the country. It was a sport jacket, but lots of men were showing up for work in them.

Despite a rush of publicity about the new suits, many retailers were skeptical that spring. But as the Nehru gathered momentum, most haberdashers shut their eyes and ordered big.

Some were caught with too many on hand when the fad died at summer's end, yet few men's clothiers made money without them in 1968.

The jacket was cut and collared like the mandarin outfits worn by Jawaharlal Nehru, the prime minister of India from 1947–64 and a symbol of peaceful Indian resistance to British rule. They were the perfect icons for emerging U.S. pacifism in the sixties and became known early on as "the Guru," "the Mandarin," or the "Meditation Coat."

Stylish stars helped spread the fad. Ken Harrelson, a slugger with the Boston Red Sox, turned up in several national magazines wearing a powder-blue Nehru. New York Jets quarterback Joe Namath prowled the night spots of Manhattan in Nehru suits.

Detroit Tiger pitcher Denny McLain, who won thirty-one games that summer, performed on the electric organ at a Detroit nightclub while wearing a $3,000 Russian White Broadtail Nehru coat, complete with a large, gold medallion.

But the real ambassador of the trend was Davis. He owned a half-dozen Nehrus (not to mention an assortment of gold chains and medallions), and he wore them everywhere—including onstage in Las Vegas.

Still, clothiers in middle America were hesitant. In early April, disagreement over the Nehru touched off a controversy at the National Association of Men's Sportswear Buyers Show at the Sheraton Atlantic Hotel in New York. The president of one garment manufacturer said, "Very few retailers will have a successful fall season unless they feature the Nehru." But not everyone agreed. Said a clothier from Connecticut, "Some of the merchandise like the Nehru is a little bit too way out. I've seen stuff in some showrooms I can't possibly sell in my store."

But the Nehru look did indeed spread out of the vanguard New York shops to men's stores throughout the country, and it appealed to all income brackets. Silton Brothers, a major Los Angeles distributor, reported sales of more than sixty thousand jackets by early May.

The coats stayed hot until late summer, when they began filling up the warehouses and backrooms of department stores and men's clothing shops. The boom went bust as Nehrus gave way to the Edwardian look, with its slim, high-cut jackets.

Some attributed the collapse to a growing number of men with the wrong physique who squeezed into the narrow-waisted jacket. Fat guys in slender-cut Nehrus, with a gleaming medallion accentuating the paunch, left a slightly comic impression.

So rapid was the decline and so acute was the overstock problem, that some clothiers took desperate measures. Harris and Frank, a large menswear chain, sewed balmacaan collars onto the Nehru coats and converted them into Edwardian suits. By October, the once ubiquitous Nehru was no longer visible on the streets of major metropolises. Only lower income buyers, unable to switch quickly to other styles, wore Nehrus that fall.

But though the mandarin jacket faded fast, it signaled a major change in American men's dress. By autumn, jaunty, showy male plumage was flourishing. A new sophisticated and ostentatious tailoring bowled over the traditional male formal fashion. It was the breakthrough that ushered in everything from wide-lapelled jackets and flared pants to colored dress shirts—all staples of menswear long after the Nehru had become a museum piece.

TIE-DYEING

Tie-Dyeing
101

Tie-dye was an old and honored craft practiced for more than a thousand years in the Far East when it caught on with the late-sixties flower generation.

A simple home-stewing procedure resulted in clothing and other fabric that fit the utilitarian, yet expressionist life style of sixties youth. The faintly geometric splotches of color and form were endlessly original and suggested the psychedelic experience derived from hallucinogenic drugs.

The hippie communities of San Francisco began do-it-yourself dyeing in 1966 and 1967 as the counterculture movement was taking shape. Rock musicians were soon wearing dye-patterned clothes onstage and by late 1969, tie-dye adorned young people throughout the country.

Tie-dyed goods could be purchased from artisans or cooked up at home. Using strands of tie string or elastic and boiling pots of dye, one could emblazon clothes, bedspreads, sheets, tablecloths, bath towels, curtains, and even create artwork suitable for framing.

Several celebrities became enthusiasts, many calling upon favorite artists who sprang from the hippie cottage industries to become tie-dyers to the stars. So widespread was the fad that by 1969, major clothing manufacturers were turning out print clothing with tie-dye designs.

The craft, known in India as *bandhnu,* consisted of tying off lengths of fabrics at intervals so that the bound area would not absorb color when dipped in dye. The result was a loosely patterned flow of color and shape. In India, the ornate fabrics were used as curtains for temple paintings, tents, screens, and costumes. Discoveries of tie-dyed material in Japan and China date back to the sixth century and are on display in museums around the world.

In the 1960's, tie-dye became a practical means of self-expression. By wrapping the cloth in any one of a number of basic ties, including pleats, marblings, rosettes, bunches, and doughnut knots, craftsmen could produce wildly varied and aesthetically pleasing designs.

Once the shapes were gathered and doused with water, the fabric was dipped in hot dye for at least twenty minutes, allowing the color to absorb everywhere but beneath the ties. After removal from the simmering liquid, the cloth was rinsed in cold running water and then pressed while still wet. The process could be repeated several times with different colors, and subtle shading was achieved by rubbing the cloth with chlorine bleach or immersing it in boiling color remover liquids.

Anyone could do it and it seemed everyone did. But there were a handful of legendary tie-dyers on either coast who concocted breathtaking designs learned through years of experimentation. They did it by skillfully using eyedroppers and spray bottles to make strategic applications of dye into bound fabric.

The most famous was "Tie-Dye Annie" Thomas, a former New York advertising copywriter who took up a hippie existence in San Francisco in 1967. At the Free Store in Haight-Ashbury, she learned how to dye secondhand clothing and was soon creating dazzling patterns for other denizens of the Haight.

Her fame spread rapidly and by 1969 she was producing commissioned tie-dye masterworks out of an unpretentious workshop in Hollywood Hills, California. With an English-born professional designer as a partner, Thomas turned out clothing for the likes of Mama Cass Elliot, The Rolling Stones, and other celebrities, but refused to capitalize in a big way. She accepted no more than $7.50 for each item that came out of her boiling vats of lye and sodium hydrosulfate.

Across the country, Will and Eileen Richardson of Manhattan gained notoriety for tie-dye designs that wound up in prestigious shops like Bonwit Teller, where a small scarf by the couple went for $40. The Richardsons worked out of their New York City studio, Up Tied, but occasionally snuck off to the island of Tobago, where they set up a portable worktable on the beach and built fires to heat their dye pots.

Fashion designer Halston made extensive use of the Richardsons' tie-dye patterns in his collections. He also dressed numerous celebrity clients in the chic new style, including red-hot actress Ali MacGraw and singer Liza Minnelli, who wore tie-dye at her Waldorf opening in February 1970.

For some artists, tie-dye was a relatively new outlet. But the craze provided overnight attention for long-time practitioners of the craft. Californian Bert Bliss had been creating wondrous patterns in his kitchen for twenty years when the tie-dye fad suddenly put him in overwhelming demand.

At the peak of the craze, some hippie households were awash in tie-dye. Everything from wall hangings and throw rugs to long johns and tennis shoes were being soaked in dye pots. Pop singer John Sebastian outfitted his entire house and body with wild flora from pots that steamed on his kitchen stove. Another famous proponent was English rock star Joe Cocker, who took the stage at Woodstock in full-dress tie-dye.

With popularity spreading to young people in every part of the country, major fabric producers like Burlington Industries were mass-producing tie-dye designs for retail stores.

Tie-dyeing was so closely linked with America's youth movement that the onset of predyed clothing was regarded by some as a sign of waffling commitment to general principles. Wrote *Newsweek* columnist Stewart Alsop in 1970, "It costs a bit more, of course, but the more affluent young revolutionaries can now buy their pants pre-tie-dyed and pre-raggedized. These pants—and much else besides—make it a little difficult to take the youth revolution so solemnly as it was once taken."

About the same time that predyed apparel arrived in department stores, the West Coast infatuation began to slip. Suddenly, after a millennium and a half, tie-dye was looking very dated.

Through the 1970's tie-dye was chiefly remembered as a sixties artifact, although the recipe was never forgotten. Indeed, a comeback seemed forever in the offing, and sure enough at the National Fashion and Boutique Show in June 1984, tie-dye was proclaimed hot again. Bloomingdale's opened a juniors boutique called Too-Dye-For, selling T-shirts, pedal pushers, and bathing suits with the familiar old designs.

There was even a revival of home-brewing, with several newspaper and magazine editors dusting off the old instructions and running them again. For kids too young to remember the sixties, tie-dye was not a symbol, but something fresh, fun, and altogether far out.

BLACK LIGHT

The early phosphorescent posters which revealed their messages only under ultraviolet light were one of
the great gimmicks of the psychedelic age. The effect was so
bedazzling—usually accompanied by squeals of delight—that it
touched off a more general "black light" craze in the late sixties.
By 1970, no college dormitory room was complete without a
purple fluorescent bulb that turned ordinary surroundings into a
phantasmagoria of radiumlike luminescence.

Black lights, along with waterbeds, burning incense, strobe
lights, and wildly surreal posters and wall hangings were part of
the decor in a typical youth haven or hippie pad of the era.
Together they added up to a classic sixties ambience.

Most youth trappings were inspired by the hallucinogenic od-
yssey. Acid rock, blurry-edged tie-dye clothing, tendrilous poster
lettering by San Francisco artists like Wes Wilson and Stanley

Mouse, Fillmore auditorium light shows, and other sixties miscellany derived from or reflected the sights and sounds of the LSD experience.

Like ancient sun worshippers, the hippie culture attached semireligious significance to the drug-induced, dreamlike swirl of color and light and surrounded themselves with the imagery. Blinking rock show strobes put performers in an eerie slow motion, color projectors bathed them in resplendent hues, and black light gave them a fluorescent sheen.

Early in the century, audiences were left spellbound by the mystery and novelty of black lights used to enliven stage productions, dance theaters, and ice-skating extravaganzas. Performers wore costumes and uniforms treated with fluorescent materials under mercury lamps producing black light.

The normal eye can see radiant energy between four hundred and seven hundred nanometers in wavelength. Black light falls in the invisible range of three hundred twenty to three hundred eighty nanometers, but a fluorescent material or chemical sensitive to such light absorbs the energy and glows at wavelengths which can be seen with the naked eye.

Black light has long been used for a variety of detection, inspection, and identification chores. Health inspectors beam ultraviolet rays to turn up tiny food deposits on cooking utensils in restaurants and urine splatter in public facilities. Fluorescent rodent droppings can be spotted in flour and grain, and sour eggs fluoresce green or blue when shuttled underneath overhead luminaires.

Ticket holders at public events are often marked with fluorescent ink to permit gate reentry, and money and valuables are sometimes sprinkled with powder that shows up on the hands of thieves when exposed to black light.

Ornamental displays are common. Black lights are used for nightclubs and restaurant murals, Christmas decorations, shop windows, and outdoor signboards.

The special effect first took on psychedelic properties during the poster craze that started in late 1966. The rage began with psychedelic rock concert advertisements and quickly spread to the colorful doodling of Peter Max and personality pinups idolizing the likes of James Dean, Humphrey Bogart, and Jean-Paul Belmondo.

Black light posters, touched up with fluorescent paints, lacquers, water colors, inks, and dyes, became part of the scene. A psychedelic fantasia, invisible under normal light, came alive when a black light bulb, purchased at one of the early head shops of 1966 and 1967, was aimed at the picture.

Posters were often sold with weak and inefficient incandescent bulbs used for short-range viewing of specific objects. But when young people began buying long, cylindrical black light fluorescent lamps, they put entire living spaces in a whole new light.

Black light parties flourished and first-time witnesses to the spectacle let out *oohs* and *ahs* as odds and ends were illuminated by ultraviolet rays. The black beam irradiated clothes washed in laundry detergent containing fluorescent phosphates as a whitening ingredient and caused teeth cleaned with the likes of monofluorophosphate toothpaste to gleam like never before.

White undershirts, a favorite outerwear among young men in the late sixties, gave off a blazing, blinding light, while girls suffered the embarrassment of having white undergarments shine through sheer dresses and blouses.

Early on, some enthusiasts took to painting their faces and hands with fluorescent materials that would show up under black light. Peace symbols, names, and a few obscenities were popular graffiti. A favorite pastime was picking luminous lint off one another's clothing.

The mania spread to high school crowds by the early seventies. Black light lamps became the rage of teenage bedrooms and touched off a stream of student science papers which sought to explain the effect.

Literally dozens of suppliers of black light equipment and fluorescent materials rushed into the new market. They not only sold bulbs, lamps, and filters, but also fluorescent paints, ink, dye, chalk, crayons, pencils, phosphors, powder, lacquer, water colors, and fabric.

Some concert halls, night spots, and restaurants sought to create a deeper psychedelic experience by using a flashing black light in conjunction with a strobe or color projector. When no form of visible light was present, a part of the eye lens which fluoresces naturally under black light caused a slightly disorienting, purple haze. The effect was said to be a visual approximation of LSD encounters when combined with a flashing light source.

But black light, for all its continuing practical uses, was the quintessence of novelty. Though it still served as a backdrop for drugs in the early seventies, excitement over glowing teeth and bright white apparel began to dim.

The effect is less dramatic in states which have since banned phosphates in laundry detergents because of their effect on the ecosystem. But lamps are still sold in poster stores and record shops and they remain popular—as popular as beanbag chairs—among college freshmen setting up housekeeping for the first time in a campus dormitory room.

MINIBIKES

Courtesy of K & P Mfg., Azusa, California

For years crafty kids had rigged up handcarts and bicycles with lawn mower or washing machine engines, then puttered around in makeshift motorized heaven.

But the fun was limited to mechanically astute wrench hands until manufactured minibikes arrived in the late 1960's. The new vehicles were pint-sized scooters intended for off-road use, but they became kingpins of suburban subdivision streets in their day.

Though skimpy and not particularly fast, minibikes were perfect for a generation of subteens too short to straddle their older brothers' motorcycles. It was a terrific toy that swiped attention from that age-old adolescent favorite—the go-cart.

Minis were part of a wave of motorbike enthusiasm that swept the country in the sixties. Cycling began to shed its Marlon Brando image with Honda's "You Meet the Nicest People on a Honda" advertising campaign, and by mid-decade biking on moderately powered two-wheelers was a relatively clean-cut diversion which won over millions.

Inevitably, manufacturers moved to satisfy youthful longing for motorized transportation. The first models were essentially factory-built versions of the venerable washing machine screamers. They were stark vehicles with lightweight tubular frames and wheels about ten inches in diameter. The bikes stood about four feet tall and weighed as little as sixty-five pounds.

Most came with the same two- and four-cycle industrial engines used in grass cutters and other power equipment. Many of the early models had no suspension, and a few were without brakes.

But the affordable minibikes were an immediate hit. By 1969 the market was filled with more than thirty manufacturers, including Rupp, Bonham, Bonanza, Benelli, Heathkit and Honda, building in excess of eighty minibike models. Sophisticated units had both front and rear braking, suspension for a smoother ride, fancy fenders, headlights and more heat under the seat, sometimes as much as five horsepower.

Millions sold in the late sixties. Many went for under $150, and the top of most lines could be purchased for less than $300. Kids everywhere had them, as subdivision streets and woods and hills adjacent to housing developments came alive with the steady snore of Briggs and Stratton and Tecumseh engines.

Comparatively little street racing went on, since the vehicles were hardly Davidson. Unless souped up by inventive older brothers, the tiny piston pushers—built to twirl lawn mower blades twice a week—could muster only touring speeds. Nor were minibikes made for rapid, tight cornering.

But if smooth surface racing was out, off-roading was definitely in. On dirt trails and through wooded paths they were wondrously tough little gimmicks that could be spun, catapulted, and crashed into small trees and come out no worse for wear.

Packs of moaning minibikes would charge up hills at the height of the craze, carving swaths into vacant properties and prompting irritated landowners to string deviously low wire to keep them off premises.

Even with hazards—both natural and man-made—back-woods trails were far more suited to minibikes than were public streets. Yet when slightly larger engines arrived, boosting some bikes up to forty miles per hour, there was a growing tendency to take them into traffic. Most states did not allow minis on public right-of-ways since they were too short to be seen by drivers of standard vehicles and frequently did not have proper brakes or lights. And even if a bike could be licensed for the road, the eleven- or twelve-year-old kids who drove them could not.

As the fad intensified in 1969, minibike safety became an overriding issue. A national outcry followed the death in early 1970 of an eleven-year-old Richmond, California, boy whose bike struck a chain stretched across a road.

At the urging of the citizenry, hundreds of police departments made minibike enforcement a priority. Kids were advised to wear helmets and protective clothing and to turn off engines and walk bikes across streets. They were also warned against trick steering, weaving, and driving at excessive speeds on wet or loose gravel surfaces.

The design and construction of the bikes also came under attack. In 1970, *Consumer Bulletin* magazine decreed that "minibikes are not safe for children and are probably not safe for adults. Too many have poorly engineered construction and are not designed with the comfort or safety of the rider in mind."

But on most American neighborhood streets, minibikes remained in full force. When cars came by they scattered like flies, darting up onto sidewalks, ducking into driveways, and then buzzing back onto the roadway when the danger had passed.

By 1969, some adults began using minibikes as on-site transportation during outdoor excursions. Campers, hunters, and fishermen loaded the squat machines into the backs of station wagons and pick-ups and carted them to secluded spots. Private airplane pilots bought them to zip quickly across airport aprons, and playground supervisors covered acres of ball diamonds in them.

By the early seventies, the first generation of adolescent minibike enthusiasts had begun to grow into motorcycles. At the same time, there arrived on the market a spate of small, street-legal motorcycles that were larger, faster, more maneuverable, and less jarring than minibikes.

By 1973 the small engines which had motorvated millions of young riders went back into lawn mowers, while newspaper classified sections filled up with used minibikes for sale.

The little two-wheelers that wouldn't sell were packed away in basements, attics, garage rafters, or disassembled for parts. Those which remained in one piece were occasionally dusted off, fed a cupful of gasoline, and scootered up the street to the nostalgic delight of one and all.

WATER BEDS

Ken Regan, Camera 5

In his quest to create the perfect chair—one that would cradle and nuzzle the human body—California furniture designer Charles Hall filled an inflatable vinyl bag with liquid starch in 1968. But when he sat in his three-hundred-pound seat, he slowly sank, plunging deeper and deeper as if being swallowed by a giant amoeba.

Next he tried gorging a bag with gelatin, but the quivering contents decomposed over time, leaving a lumpy semiliquid. Undaunted, Hall hit upon the right stuffing when he pumped water into a hard plastic sack and turned his formfitting chair into the water bed.

There were still problems to overcome. For instance, when the water cooled, his bed felt like an ice pack—quite literally sending shivers up the spine. But a radiant heat unit solved the problem, and Hall was on his way to making furniture and fad history.

By 1970 water beds were introduced to counterculture acclaim and soon found mainstream enthusiasts as well. For months they were a national novelty, and the water-bed industry has survived long after the craze days ended.

The idea of furniture conforming to the human shape began with the beanbag. But Hall sought a substance that would give with each movement and snuggle every contour of the body. The water sack hugged and soothed the physique with hypnotic pitch and roll. Water made for a gentle sloshing motion and produced a sound that turned the cushion into a relaxant. But the sensation was better suited for reclining than sitting, so Hall forgot about the chair and built a bed instead.

He outfitted the vinyl bunk with a safety liner, placed it in a frame, attached a thermostat and heating element, and spent a year and a half trying to interest manufacturers. Finally, King Koil Sleep Products agreed to place the first water beds into production.

The beds went on sale in the summer of 1970 and quickly became a retail phenomenon. Store model displays became trendy gathering places as shoppers waited for a chance to lie down on a water bed and fall fast afloat.

A customer in a Minneapolis department store reportedly drifted off to sleep after stretching out on a floor model. But the scene was livelier at other water-bed displays. At Bloomingdale's in New York, the water-bed showcase area was said to have been a meeting place for singles.

A bevy of manufacturers and distributors with names like Innerspace Environments, Aquarius Products, The Water Works, Aqua Beds, and The Wet Dream entered the surging water-bed market. Within six months of their introduction more than fifteen thousand beds had sold, and demand was far outdistancing supply.

The units caught on first with alternative life-stylists, becoming standard in hippie pads, along with black lights, burning incense, and psychedelic posters. But water beds also appealed to a fast-living moneyed set typified by *Playboy* magazine publisher Hugh Hefner, who bought a king-sized version for his Chicago mansion and covered it with a Tasmanian opossum spread. They were installed in luxury suites of Las Vegas hotels as a symbol of a new hedonism, and even some large motel chains considered water beds the wave of the future and began placing large orders with manufacturers.

The beds ranged in price from $30 for a simple bladder mattress to $2,800 for designer Aaron Donner's lavish Pleasure Island model, sold by Innerspace. The eight-foot-square water wonderland included matching pillows, an attached sound system and television set, directional lighting, and, of course, a wet bar.

Much of the curiosity stemmed from the alleged sexual benefits promoted by several companies. Aquarius claimed in ads that "two things are better on a water bed. One of them is sleep." Another company promised that owners would "live and love in liquid luxury."

But water beds were also praised for their lulling and even healing powers. Devotees claimed that lying on a water mattress cured insomnia and eased back problems.

The fear of houses being flooded by leaky water beds proved unfounded. Water could not escape rapidly unless a large gash was somehow torn in the hard vinyl skin. Patch kits similar to those used to repair bicycle tires were kept handy in case of a puncture.

The biggest headache was caused by the sheer weight. Many tipped the scales at more than three quarters of a ton, and there were reports of beds in old houses causing upstairs floors to sag. A bed that sprang a leak in California was pushed onto a balcony that promptly collapsed under the weight. One new owner testing his bed in the backyard for leaks watched it suddenly gather momentum and slowly roll downhill—bowling over shrubbery and gardens before easing to a halt.

But it was loss of novelty, rather than occasional tragicomedy, which caused the fad to falter in the early 1970's. Yet a genuine water-bed industry was left in its wake. In 1984, the Waterbed Manufacturers Association reported that 17 percent of all beds purchased were water beds. Meanwhile, some of the claims of health benefits were being confirmed.

A 1975 report in the *American Family Physician* showed that decubitus ulcers, or bedsores, could be alleviated by having long-term hospital patients sleep on water beds. The undulations allow a flow of air between body and mattress and reduce stress on pressure points.

Several hospitals began using water mattresses for immobile patients, including the elderly and persons suffering from strokes, severe burns, and orthopedic problems.

Water beds received another boost when some physicians suggested that they improve blood circulation—something any zealot knew in 1970. The once-trendy aqua beds were no longer a fad but were still a good idea.

HOT PANTS

Julian Wasser

Hot Pants

Paris designers were going to exasperating new lengths with hemlines in 1970 and American women were unhappy.

After years of wearing skirts above and beyond the knee, they were holding out for something shorter than the midi skirt. So when "hot pants" arrived in January 1971, to carve a niche outside the mainstream, U.S. buyers created a runaway smash.

In one unprecedented burst of fashion will, women rebelled against Paris and the midi and went for a higher, tighter, and flashier version of the fifties "short-shorts." The time was right for hot pants, which offered a sexy shock appeal even the long-reigning mini skirt could not match.

Hot pants happened so fast that boutiques and department stores struggled for weeks to catch up. Despite intense cold in many areas, shoppers everywhere were trying them, buying them, and wearing them home beneath long overcoats. Though originally targeted for the spring market, hot pants were a coast-to-coast fad by February 1.

The long forecasted midi skirt invasion was said to be at hand in late 1970, although sales in the United States remained slow. Such was opposition to lower hemlines that organized anti-midi groups sprang up. Girls Against More Skirt (GAMS) and Fight Against Dictating Designers (FADD) exemplified an unyielding spirit. In the fall of 1970, the president of Bonwit Teller in Manhattan suggested that female sales personnel don midis to help consumers adjust to life below the knee. But retail houses grew increasingly nervous and were ready to jump on the hot pants bandwagon as soon as it began to roll.

"The way women are buying and men are reacting it would seem legs have been out of sight for ten years, not ten months," said one Manhattan boutique owner when the shorts began to take hold.

Hot pants, so named in the pages of *Women's Wear Daily*, were first spotted on London's King's Road and the sidewalks of

Paris's St.-Germain-des-Prés. In London they stopped at the top of the thigh and in Paris they settled at mid-thigh.

In New York, the pants got hot with the smart set. The streets of Manhattan became a giant cheesecake walk led by dozens of dropped names. Jackie Onassis, Marlo Thomas, and Mrs. Robert Stack were seen boulevarding in thigh-tops. Ursula Andress was spotted dining out in a pair of bronze velvet hot pants and Raquel Welch, Hollywood's leading lady at the time, had a special pair made to take on location in Spain.

Cold weather seemed to intensify the fad. Hot pants and long boots beneath an overcoat became a stunning symbol of winter, 1971. The high and tight shorts hinted at warmer times and dramatized the lengths to which women would go to avoid the confounded midi skirt.

They became acceptable attire for everything from grocery shopping to black tie dinners. Women stepped out of sleek limos with hot pants and stood in ravishing contrast to floor-length gowns at formal engagements.

A New York socialite explained that she wore them "because it's so nice to show legs again. It's 1971 and shorts are contemporary, and I think people are depressed by the old-looking midi-skirts." Said one model and proponent, "You can sit how you like and walk upstairs without everyone going 'wow.'"

The pants came in every conceivable color and fabric and were worn in a variety of lengths—from Bermuda style over the knee to the upper reaches of the thigh. But they were uniformly tight and well-tucked.

Satin and leather were popular, but no material was off limits. One New York furrier reported selling several pairs of $195 ranch mink hot pants, though his green monkey fur shorts were less successful. Elsewhere, hot pants were being fashioned out of chiffon, silk, denim, and broadcloth. They came studded with rhinestones or sprinkled with glitter.

Hot pants were a sales success from one side of the country to the other, and not just in fashion centers. With the coming of spring they declined with the haute couture, but many women were just warming up to them.

So widespread was the fad that the usual bastions of clothing conservatism were forced to give ground. Countless employers had to decide whether hot pants constituted appropriate work apparel, and most wound up in the affirmative. In September, the chairman of the Miss America pageant dropped the contest's ban on hot pants, allowing participants to wear them during the talent competition. "They are the sort of fad that topples institutions," observed one fashion expert.

Explanations for the phenomenon were rampant. Most saw it as a rebellion against dictatorial Paris designers. Others saw a continuation of the permissive sixties. "They are an expression of the female's new freedom and they mean she is no longer willing to be submissive to convention," said Dr. Jason Miller, a New York psychiatrist. "They also show that she is on a serious mission to relate to other people—especially men. She may not be wearing them just to be sexually provocative, but because she desires to get attention as a prelude to a genuine relationship."

Hot pants, which were variously known as Cool Pants, Shortcuts, Les Shorts, Happy Legs, and Shortootsies, were also viewed as part nostalgia for the short pants worn by Ruby Keeler, Deanna Durbin, and other screen symbols of the 1930's and 1940's. At the time of the hot pants craze, Keeler was enjoying a revival on Broadway with *No, No Nanette:* There was a sprinkling of other fashion trends rooted in her movie heyday, including deep-red lipstick, hair ornaments, chokers, and the wide-shoulder look.

Whatever the inspiration, hot pants continued selling through summer. But by fall it was clear that American women were not prepared to wear them through another cold season.

There were no complaints along fashion row when the fad died. It had been a boffo nine months and industry experts later theorized that hot pants had given American women one last bare-legged fling and had readied them psychologically for the mid-length skirts of the 1970's.

SMILE BUTTONS

The peace symbol of the seventies? The post-hippie sign of jolly good fellowship? Why, the smile button, of course.

It may have been the simplest insignia of all time—a pair of black beady eyes set over a sweeping smile inside a noseless circle. But it was irresistible to millions of Americans in 1971.

Smile buttons were a mirth-andising marvel—so ubiquitous it was ridiculous. The turned-up mouth turned up on everything from T-shirts to toilet seats, but it appeared mostly as a big beaming button that sold for anywhere from fourteen cents to one dollar.

It was a fad that swept the country without a lot of media bombast; the face was suddenly everywhere, like a radiant, benevolent Big Brother. No one knew where it came from, and few seemed to care. But in a confrontational age, the great happy visage stood for something with which everyone could agree. It was the first apolitical, asexual, noncontroversial button.

After fading quietly away the face made a comeback in the mid-seventies, this time with the circle yellowed-in and the chipper phrase "Have a Nice Day" stringing alongside. But the short-lived "Nice Day" expression was soon a target for comedians and social commentators. The line was taken as a meaningless valediction, and the famed linear smile passed for blithering idiocy.

N. G. Slater, a New York button manufacturer, began producing the happy face in 1969. The Smilie, as it was first known, was introduced during a general enthusiasm for witty, ribald, often startling buttons worn by young people. At first, Smilie was lost in the button shuffle. It may not have been strident enough for 1969, but by the spring of 1971, the happy face had become everyone's favorite put-on. The nation broke out in a smile button craze, and then the silly grin began appearing on dozens of other items. Anything bearing the face was a happy hot seller. It was stamped on necklaces, cuff links, lighters, lamps, rugs, purses, stationery, coffee cups, writing pads, dolls, even trash cans. Cartier in New York offered golden smiles made to order.

Cheerfulness was suddenly the image everyone wanted to convey. Early bird presidential candidate George McGovern used the smile button as a campaign logo, and Good Humor ice cream and countless retail stores across the country adopted the smile theme. The nation's biggest smile exhorted travelers to "See Rock City" on Lookout Mountain in Tennessee.

Sales of smile items were sensational. A Philadelphia novelty-maker called Traffic Stoppers sold at least thirty different smile products in 1971 and racked up $1 million in sales within six months of the fad's spring takeoff. Slater filled huge orders for buttons, like one for five hundred thousand from F. W. Woolworth, and wound up selling several million that year.

There seemed no limit to the number of smiling faces Americans were willing to buy. By early fall it was estimated that more than twenty million buttons alone had sold, representing almost one American out of ten. Not since the Hula Hoop had any U.S. fad penetrated as deeply as the smile button.

Few people attached much significance to the smile. When asked to comment by *The New York Times,* famous Los Angeles psychologist Dr. Arthur Janov passed, saying, "It is hardly one of the burning issues of the day."

But the most famous smile since Mona Lisa's became a media plaything, including a deadly armament in the hands of political caricaturists. Both *Newsweek* and *Time* printed a cartoon illustrating differences between President Nixon and AFL-CIO president George Meany by showing Nixon with a smile button and Meany with a scowl button.

Nurses everywhere wore them to light up sick wards, waitresses began signing restaurant checks with quickly drawn smiling faces, and merry graffiti artists took to filling up any blank circular shape with eyes and an upturned mouth.

Not surprisingly, smile satirists moved into action. Among the spin-offs were faces with toothy grins and faces with tongues lolling out of their mouths from exhaustion.

Just who drew it was never satisfactorily determined, although many laid claim. According to one story which got national play, New York radio station WMCA—home of the popular "Good Guys"—had used a similar face as part of a station promotion a few years earlier. They were plastered on sweat shirts handed out from 1964–66, and a few were still being seen around town at the height of the smile button craze.

For years, people had been decorating personal correspondence with similarly sparse happy faces, and the tradition may have simply grown into the limelight. But one way or another, a smiling face which came out of N. G. Slater's design department became a national motif.

The buttons continued to sell into 1972. The new smile consciousness in America even prompted *The New Yorker* to lead off its May 27 "Talk of the Town" section with the observation that "America is waking up once again to the importance of plain old smiling." It noted that "smile buttons are moving fast, so incurable sourpusses can pull their weight, too."

Just as the country grew accustomed to the face, it began to recede. But in its regenerated form, as a yellow button accompanied by the "Have A Nice Day" slogan, it came in for some brickbatting. By the late seventies the unremitting refrain was driving the nation bonkers. Every retail purchase, every casual conversation, every form of human interplay—no matter the tone or temperament—seemed punctuated with the same send-off: "Have A Nice Day."

The line was the butt of stand-up monologues, and the smile button became the face that launched a thousand quips. Dozens of enterprising comics at hip clubs like the Comedy Store in Los Angeles were doing wise-guy facial impressions of a smile button.

The broad smile—now turning up on balloons, license plates, and huge municipal water tanks—had turned into the universal image of benign indifference. Its gleam was reduced to a cheery obliviousness that became a favorite, if overused, symbol for the likes of movie directors and naturalist photographers.

Under attack, buttons and other smile products began to disappear from knickknack shelves. Many millions of buttons sold in the seventies were shut away in bottom drawers or released as used goods to flea markets.

The great goofy grin went underground, waiting for Americans to rise up, as they had in 1971, in a spirit of congeniality. Indeed, when the "Nice Day" backlash finally died down, in the early eighties the irrepressible smile buttons began popping up again on a few lapels. To a much smaller degree, happy days were back again.

BODY TATTOOS

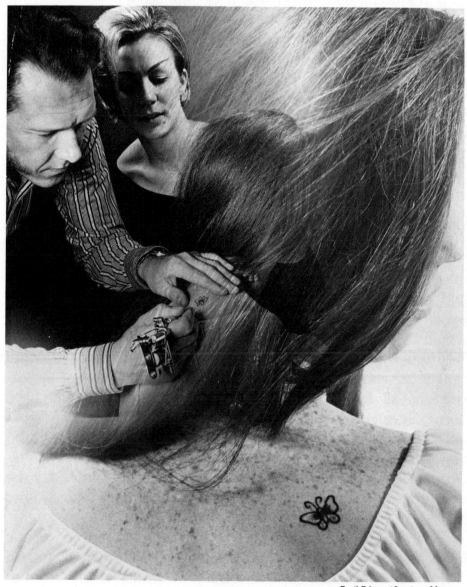

Emil Edgren/*San Jose Mercury*

Body Tattoos

125

When a wave of hip, young celebrities went in for body tattoos in the late sixties, they helped crack an age-old social barrier. Before that time tattooing had been a sin against skin, a seedy self-abasement reserved for motorcycle gang members and World War II vintage sailors.

But with stellar endorsement, everlasting body tattoos became widely accepted, if not exactly chic. Young women in particular were anxious to have their skin indelibly inked with delicate flowers and butterflies.

The little beauties were only skin-deep, but that was enough. The tattooed could not afford to say they were sorry, because neither folk remedies nor modern techniques like skin abrasion and laser surgery were entirely effective ways to erase that part of your past.

Tattooing was an irreversible act, the one fad you couldn't put away. As such, conscientious artists during the early seventies craze made sure—doubly sure—that clients were ready, willing, and sober. Regrets? There've been a few. Just ask the marked men and women who today wear long-sleeved shirts and blouses in summer or show discolored blotches on their hands and ankles with still recognizable outlines of tattoos that wouldn't go away.

Though practiced for centuries in various cultures, tattooing caught on with American sailors in the 1940's. Once discharged, veterans all told the same story to friends and family back home. Several carousing crew members were in a port town bar one night when someone got the bright idea of visiting a tattoo parlor. They came away with MOTHER inscribed on their shoulders or the name of a sweetheart that would one day be obscured by a serpent, a flag, a nude woman, or some other intricately drawn camouflage of forgotten love.

Tattooing was adopted next by motorcycle madmen of the fifties and sixties, who emblazoned skull and bones, winged skeletons, and defiant expressions like "Born to Lose," "Born to Raise Hell," and "Death Before Dishonor" on their skin.

But body markings were not nefarious in the Age of Aquarius. Pop artists like Cher, Joan Baez, and Grace Slick of Jefferson Airplane had feminine icons etched on their bodies. But the most famous tattoo belonged to Janis Joplin, whose left breast bore a red heart. The wave of celebrity tattooing spurred the "living jewelry" fad. Tattooists were suddenly boosted in stature from sleaze entrepreneurs to genuine artists who engraved designs onto living canvases.

Much of the action was in California, but by early 1972 young women all over the country were getting tattooed all over their bodies. They tattooed midriffs near the bikini line. They tattooed the small of the back, the ankle, the back of the hand, the earlobe, and hidden extremities which emphasized the partly sexual nature of the fad.

Besides butterflies and flora, they chose sunbursts, varieties of fish, people and place names, and occasionally upbeat mottoes. Males preferred symbols of freedom and fancifulness over motorcycle gang morbidity. The role model was actor Peter Fonda, who wore a dolphin on his shoulder.

The cost of tattooing varied depending on the intricacy of the design, the number of colors used, and the location. A small flower or butterfly on the shoulder cost from $15 to $40. For an ornate back mural that stretched from neckline to belt line, you could pay up to $5,000.

The most famous tattoo artist was Lyle Tuttle, whose media stardom in the early seventies was in part because virtually every square inch of his body—save for face, hands and feet—was covered with a wild rococo of dense, detailed, modern tattooing. He looked like the exterior of a hippie van sprung to life.

He was a shocking sight who frequently turned up in national magazines alongside female clients with similar bodies eccentric. Few fadsters went in for Tuttle's full-dress tattoos, but they flocked to his studio to have their skin memorialized in some small way by the master.

The method of Tuttle and other modern tattoo artists was less painful than the old system of punch and dye. The new tattooing was done with an electric ink and needle machine that pricked the skin sixty times a second and left one of several colors of India Ink imbedded forever in the epidermis.

Once dipped in dye, the tattoo machine would be traced

over a design drawn on the skin with a ballpoint pen. The new system was not painless, but was far less unpleasant than the ritual of puncturing that was once part of a sailor's passage into manhood.

However, the new tattoos were just as permanent as the old ones, a fact which seemed to intensify the thrill of having it done. A rosebud on the rump would forever testify to one's impetuous youth.

When the fad began to fade in 1973, the tattoos didn't, leading to a few anguished attempts to undo what frivolous nature had done. Indeed, many were surprised to find that, like their tattoos, neither had the old social taboo against them entirely gone away.

It helped that most located their markings more discreetly than sailors once did and that illustrations were generally less offensive than in the earlier era. But as the brandished ones more and more found themselves in professional settings such as job interviews, even gentle insignias proved embarrassing.

At the peak of the tattoo binge there were impermanent alternatives. Transitory tattoos called "Skin Sees" were dye-transfer patches that came off with cold cream or nail polish remover. There was even a skintight Lyle Tuttle body shirt that replicated the rich detail of his handiwork.

Meanwhile, the truly tattooed could never wash away the evidence. But they could take a lifetime of pride in the innocence and adventure of youth.

JAZZED-UP JEANS

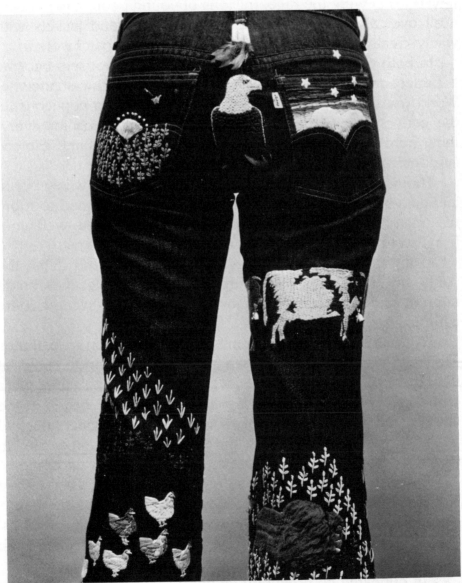

Levi's Denim Art Contest

Jazzed-Up Jeans
129

When bobby sox and blue jeans became popular in the 1940's, there was a small group of teenage girls who personalized their pants.

Almost a quarter-century later, when faded, flared, and frayed jeans were the rage, millions of young people were doing it all over again. They jazzed up jean pants and jackets with wildly creative sewing, studding, painting, and patchwork.

In both cases, plain, unprettied blue denim trousers became a perfect mode of ambulatory expression. In the shadow of World War II, blue jean artwork consisted mostly of pop icons. In the early seventies, jeans became message boards for everything from drug culture slogans to deeply personal and esoteric symbolism.

Though never really out of style, jeans became wildly popular again in 1971 as youth in the age of dissent turned to more utilitarian dress. Everyone wore "grubbies" and faded, well-worn jeans were at the heart of the unisex threadbare ethic.

In the days before designer jeans, the older and dirtier the pants, the better. Stiff, new denim was impossible. Kids broke them in as they would a ball-glove, and the pants became more companions than clothing.

To get a skintight fit, millions sat with jeans on in bathtubs filled with warm water, and then sunbathed in them to cook out the blue dye. Once blue jeans were made informal, they were embellished with patches and pictures. The trend began in the late sixties when hundreds of thousands of youngsters painted peace symbols on their pants. But as blue jean sales boomed in the new decade kids grew more inventive with their decorations.

The most memorable hippie mottoes, including "Make Love Not War," "Have a Marijuana," and "Peace Brother" (over hands clasped in a powershake), were regenerated as jean patches. Upside-down American flags were a favorite, especially in such irreverent locales as the seat of the pants.

But dungaree commentary tended to be more drug-oriented than political. The most common blue jean emblems were the leafy hemp plant that signified marijuana and the sailor from a famous brand of rolling paper. Teens also wore patches for commercial products (especially beers and soft drinks) and Boy and Girl Scout badges they'd earned just a few years before.

But aside from patching on ready-made icons, the blue jean children of the seventies let their imaginations run wild with paints, dyes, beads, and thread. Young girls sewed hearts and flowers on front pockets and back thighs or accented cuffs and inner and outer seams with colorful embroidery. The names and phone numbers of boyfriends were frequently stitched or studded above the knee, and several appliquéd the face of a loved one on the back of a jean jacket.

A Brooklyn girl told *The New York Times* in June of 1972 that a small lemon was sewn onto the knee of her favorite jeans because that's what friends thought she resembled. A teenage boy said a small suede heart stitched just below one knee of his trousers was in memory of a girlfriend who died. A leather circle with a blue rhinestone in the middle represented the moon, and a black patch of wool above one knee symbolized the young man's beard.

Rhinestone studding became a popular way to set off seams and pant bottoms, while kids who could draw applied light-colored paints to denim and created fanciful skyscapes that ran up an entire pant leg.

Patches, painting, and sewing on jeans became as important a part of wearing blue denim as shrinking and fading them. High school home economics classes became blue jean sewing circles. The rash of retail trouser outlets which sprang up carried extensive patch collections and sold thread and paint for adding the right personal touches.

As original as some of the artwork was, it was no more creative than what bobby soxers had done more than twenty-five years earlier. Blue denim slacks, saddle oxfords, and sloppy shirttails had made a big splash in the forties. Jeans were rolled up almost to the knee, but the unrolled portion was fair game for oil painting. The most common images then were highball glasses and packs of Camel cigarettes, but brush-wielding girls also drew animals, dancing couples, and likenesses of boyfriends.

One difference between the two eras: The forties kids

couldn't wear their handiwork to class, while public school dress codes had largely bowed to blue jeans—even slickered-up versions—by 1972.

Decorated pants became so popular that beginning in 1972, several top boutiques began selling high-priced denim jeans and jackets with rhinestones and jeweled designs. In 1973, Levi Strauss & Company sponsored a denim design contest that drew almost ten thousand entries. The seventy-five winners were later exhibited at New York's Museum of Contemporary Crafts and dozens of other museums around the world.

Jeans will probably always be a staple of youth fashion. But though kids still wore them in 1974, they had stopped adding patches and pictures and other adornments. Closets were suddenly lined with unfettered jeans that weren't necessarily blue. Even faded jeans began to fade away as a mindset which eventually accepted shiny new designer styles began to take shape.

TANK TOPS

Bill Eppridge, *Life* Magazine © 1969 Time Inc.

Tank Tops

Watkins Glen, New York, in July 1973, was not only the last great Woodstock era rock festival, it may have been the largest one-time/one-place congregation of tank top jerseys in the history of casual clothes.

Of the more than six hundred thousand young people who saw The Grateful Dead, The Band, and the Allman Brothers rocking in rare form, half were half-naked and the other half wore sleeveless T-shirts. Even musicians appeared in the cutaway symbol of America's fiercely informal youth dress code that summer.

Tank tops, an open-shoulder version of the basic model T-shirt, caught on with young women first, then developed unisex appeal. The name, of course, derived from the swim clothing of an earlier era, when pools were "tanks" and even male swimmers wore tops.

Millions sold, either as muscle shirts, pop tops with slogans or cartoon characters, numeralized basketball jersey lookalikes, or rock star glitter suits. There were even dress versions that could be worn anywhere in the days of tank top ubiquity.

Several pop culture versions were available, including shirts with clenched fists and Superman insignias bespeaking the Women's Liberation movement. But most were cotton, solid color tops with no comment.

Americans had been dressing down since the late sixties, and the trend peaked in 1973. A new term, "grubbies," referred to functional, unpretentious, downright sloppy garments you could deposit in your closet without hanging up. They were true clothes for comfort.

Flimsy tanks were first worn by young women in both Europe and North America. The tops were part of the no-brassiere experimentation of the day and frequently were spotted with platform shoes during the clog craze of 1972.

The style eventually went unisex and by 1973 it seemed that more American men were wearing tank tops than women.

There were plenty of role models. Mark Farner, guitarist and singer for Grand Funk Railroad, the most popular touring rock act of the early seventies, showed off his rippling musculature by striking power chords in a sleeveless shirt.

Legendary Allman Brothers bassist Berry Oakley wore a red tank top with Indian beads for the cover of the band's second album, and two members of Steely Dan had them on for the back cover of the group's landmark *Countdown To Ecstasy* album.

Working-class tanks were more likely to show beer or soft drink logos than messages of social significance. Meanwhile, rock cultists in 1973 began appliquéing all manner of flickering luminents as the glitter craze took hold in major urban centers.

Ultimately, the rhinestone-studded and sequined shirts, said to reflect big city teenage decadence, swept the hinterlands and brightened tanks and jeans everywhere by early 1974.

On the West Coast, tighter-fitting muscle shirt versions—often made of nylon—served as beachwear well before the craze caught up with the rest of the country. The showcasing of biceps, broad shoulders, and flat bellies was California body-consciousness at its best.

Tank tops were only one part of an overall surge in T-shirt acceptance. After years of declining popularity, the cotton under-shirt for men had staged a comeback in 1970 as an outergar-ment for both men and women. The new under/outerwear was everywhere, laden with topical wisecracks (dubbed T-shirt jour-nalism), pro-marijuana messages, antiwar slogans, patriotic re-joinders, and such cartoon characters as Donald Duck, Road Runner, Superman and, most predominately, Mickey Mouse. They came in all colors and in several different styles, ranging from traditional white skivvies to long-sleeved shirts favored in the cold north.

But the old-fashioned white sleeveless undershirt eventually emerged as one of the most beloved new forms of cotton outer-wear. The updated version, though, featured wider straps and an assortment of colors and prints.

Not only young people were taken with tank tops. Physical laborers of all ages were donning the air-conditioned shirts dur-ing the hot summer of 1973, and plenty of adults saw them as suitable evening dress if the evening was spent in a movie-house, a saloon, a bowling alley, or a menu-less restaurant. Going out on the town? Just tuck in your tank top and cake on deodorant.

By the following summer, tank tops, along with other T-shirt styles and blue jeans, had begun to subside. By mid-decade they were not only passé, they were a national cliché for slovenliness in a new era of dressing up. Through the remainder of the seventies, the tank top was regarded as a beer-swilling uniform, on a social scale with torn undershirts.

The style made a brief comeback among women during the California roller skating binge of the late seventies and has not died out altogether. Strapped shirts made of mesh material have been particularly popular in recent years.

What happened to the tank top ethic? The kids who wore them grew up. They made up the heart of the baby boom population, and in one short span millions moved into the ranks of the gainfully employed. The tanks were as casual and comfortable as ever, but of no use to America's emerging professional class.

EATING GLASS

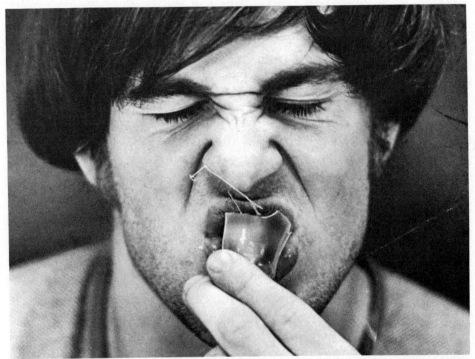

Timothy Carlson

Tim Rossovich, a raving madcap of the first order, began eating glass while an All-America defensive end at Southern Cal in the late sixties. But it wasn't until becoming an All-Pro linebacker with the Philadelphia Eagles that his odd ritual became widely known.

Rossovich's willingness to bite down on beer mugs and light bulbs was a kind of eccentricity that made him a folk hero, a football player so mean he would as soon swallow you (and your eyewear) as look at you.

But the myth was tarnished some when in 1973 a group of skeptical Harvard students tried eating glass and found it surprisingly agreeable. The school that thirty-four years earlier produced the first undergraduate to swallow a live goldfish now had students who could eat the bowl.

Rossovich, with his Rasputin stare and Harpo Marx hair, built a legend around himself with all manner of crackpot nonconformist behavior. At USC, he drove motorbikes off piers, leaped from sorority house rooftops, did headstands with his head submerged in a bucket of water, and put dents in lockers by ramming them with his noggin.

He also devoured glass during his stay at Sigma Chi house, but it didn't get reported until he was sitting in a bar one night a few years later with some Eagles teammates.

Rossovich and tight end Mike Ditka, himself quite an adventurer, were opening bottles of beer with their teeth. Well ahead in the contest, Rossovich went into his Captain Crunch routine by breaking a bottle and eating bits of glass. Ditka withdrew from the contest and Rossovich, picking ground glass from his teeth, was declared the winner. The story spread quickly and helped introduce Rossovich, who later became a professional actor, to the national media.

Eating glass supposedly meant Rossovich was tough, but in the spring of 1973 Harvard sophomore Jay Bennett, a fullback on the Crimson football team, set out to prove otherwise. He deemed glass consumption not all it was cracked up to be and declared that it had nothing to do with orneriness or any other nail-spitting traits attributed to Rossovich.

Furthermore, the young Harvard gridder meant to prove it himself. So after a few drinks at a campus party one night, a glassy-eyed Bennett removed the bulb from a nearby lamp and began to eat it.

He had called Rossovich's bluff and demystified the great gastronomic feat. But Bennett didn't stop there. Over the next few days he swallowed several more light bulbs, as did many of his friends. Soon dozens of Harvard men were feasting on bulbs. The lights went down all over Cambridge—for dessert, between meals, for midnight snacks.

Word moved fast, especially after a story about the fad

appeared in *Time* magazine. Glass eaters emerged at several eastern schools, recalling the campus-hopping craziness that followed Lothrop Withington, Jr.'s swilling of the first live goldfish in the freshman dining room at Holworthy Hall in March 1939. An attentive media helped take the fad even further and by late spring, 1973, college students in several locales around the country were eating light food.

Actually, glass eaters bore a closer resemblance to a 1939 goldfish guzzling spin-off—eating phonograph records. A University of Chicago student named John Patrick began that binge by chewing and swallowing two and a half Victrola discs, without the labels, in April 1939.

Patrick and latter-day glass eaters went about their business in much the same way. To ingest a light bulb, students first removed the filament and socket screw from an incandescent bulb and then chewed small pieces of glass until they were reduced to a fine powder. The swallowed remains reportedly had no taste, although some embellished the dish with salad dressing or granola bits.

Campus authorities were uncomfortable with the whole thing, just as they had been in 1939. Back then, the U.S. Public Health Service officials warned that goldfish might contain tapeworms that could lodge in the intestinal tract and cause anemia. The new faddists were advised that sharp bits of bulb were apt to remain in the intestines or perhaps perforate the bowel, making a hazard of passing glass. Harvard's squeamish dean of students, Archie Epps III, carried the warning to Bennett and a fellow glass-eater in May 1973. Bennett professed to be unconcerned, but everyone else soon got the message.

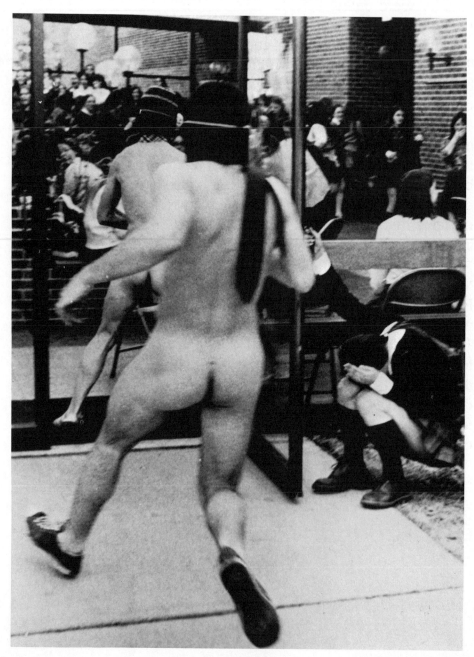

UPI/Bettmann Archive

STREAKING

One of the oddest and least modest fads of all time was streaking, the great undergraduate fun run of 1974.

It was a gag that had the whole country talking and gawking that spring. Even Richard Nixon, mired in the darkest days of his presidency, couldn't resist a playful reference to the craze. Asked at a press conference about the graying of his temples, he grinned and replied, "They call it streaking."

To streak was to dart conspicuously through a public place while dressed to the nines in nothing. Once the weather turned warm, streaking struck across the country. Hardly a school commencement exercise in America went off without incident, and there were flashes of flesh at big league baseball games, legislative assemblies, and even the Academy Award ceremonies.

Naked came the strangers, by the thousands, and they kept coming until the shock value finally wore off in June. During the last days of the craze, heads scarcely turned at the sight of yet another dashing derriere.

The fad started on campuses in southern California and Florida during a winter of growing recession, Watergate, and mountainous snow in the north. Florida State University in Tallahassee was a particularly active strip joint. Students there streaked wherever people gathered. They sped stark naked through classroom lectures, dormitories, sports events, and eventually the streets of Tallahassee.

There was so much of it going on that by early February the campus newspaper was ignoring new incidents. But media elsewhere converged on the campus and told the naked truth. The entire country soon had a nude awakening.

In the early days of the sensation, before onlookers quite knew what was happening, streaks were brief and to a point—from point A to point B as fast as the barebacks could run. Kids jumped out of hiding places such as cars stopped at traffic lights and then sprinted to a designated place of refuge. Later on, participants did not streak so much as they cavorted in large, unclothed packs while seeking others to join them.

But the dashing could be dangerous. At a restaurant in Detroit, two male streakers were charging through a pattern of tables so fast that they accidentally collided. One was knocked senseless and had to be dragged off by his partner.

There were even a few streaking tragedies. A man was killed trying to cross the Dallas-Fort Worth Turnpike, and another drowned after streaking the Queen Mary in Long Beach, California, and then diving into eighty feet of water.

But for the most part it was harmless fun, although a few bluenoses were mortified at what they viewed as a wave of public indecency. Some college administrators, like those at Yale, took disciplinary measures against streakers who were identified.

Yet the majority of campus officials figured that if left alone, the fad would die of its own excesses. Indeed, streaking eventually worked its way out of America's system, but not until a couple of months of unprecedented madness had passed.

In early March streaking arrived on a national scale. Stories rolled in from every campus in the country. A group of Harvard students zipped through a first-year anatomy class wearing nothing but surgical masks, while a streaker at the University of South Carolina raced into a campus library and asked to check out *The Naked Ape*. A student government committee at the University of Maine was discussing ways to curb streakers when one burst into the room. Several dozen nude University of Tennessee students paraded down Cumberland Avenue in Knoxville in one of the first community streaks, while out of uniform cadets at the U.S. Military Academy at West Point bucked for private by charging around buck naked with angry officers in pursuit.

The first female streaker was Laura Barton, an eighteen-year-old freshman at Carleton College in Minnesota, but by late

March coeducational streaking was commonplace. A gaggle of forty or so naked male students from Columbia University dashed the women's dormitories at Barnard College, trying to coax female companionship. They failed the first night but succeeded the next. At the University of Missouri, fifteen co-eds answered the call of thirty-five male streakers lingering beneath their dorm windows, emerging in nature's garb to go their own way.

The rah-rah spirit on campuses spread to the University of Alaska, where they ran in subzero temperatures. At Texas Tech in Lubbock, a group of students streaked for five hours to set an endurance record, while University of Georgia bare-achutists dropped from an airplane into a cheering throng and then repeated the trick a day later for cameras.

Undergraduates streaked in the same loony manner that college kids once crammed themselves into phone booths and staged panty raids. But the craze got even crazier when it spread off campus and caught on with the citizenry-at-large.

On March 12, a hairdresser in Hawaii named Gary Rogers was arrested and charged with open lewdness after running naked on the floor of the state legislature's lower chamber and declaring himself "streaker of the house." A male nudist surprised NBC's *The Tonight Show* during taping, but the incident never made it on the air that evening. Robert Opel dashed in the background while actor David Niven was at the podium at the Academy Awards, prompting Niven's famous quip about the streaker's "shortcomings."

Fearing some streaker would violate television's taboo against frontal nudity, directors of live broadcasts were on special alert. Several streaking episodes occurred on local television, although cameras were always turned away.

The fad was pandemic and no event was immune. A male streaker appeared onstage during the April 11 performance of the National Ballet of Canada in Milwaukee. Rudolf Nureyev said the streaker had a "beautiful body." On April 26, five persons wearing only Nixon masks ran through the crowd at an impeachment rally in Washington, D.C.

In Portsmouth, Rhode Island, on May 15, several Boston police officers allegedly streaked a motel lobby while in town to march in a National Police Week parade. Back in Boston, the police commissioner ordered a full probe of the incident.

In Lakeland, Florida, Chesterfield Harvey Smith and a friend were ordered to appear in court on a charge of indecent exposure after streaking a pancake house. Smith was due to be represented in court by his father, American Bar Association president Chesterfield Smith.

While the U.S.A. was under siege, the phenomena spread to other countries—often courtesy of Americans abroad. On March 11, Taiwanese police banned streaking and warned that violators would be severely punished. Four days later a group of American soldiers in South Korea went on a naked rampage, prompting police there to announce that streakers could be jailed up to twenty-nine days.

In Paris, thirteen persons streaked the Eiffel Tower; in Rome, three Americans dashed naked through St. Peter's Square; and a young Western diplomat streaked an embassy dinner party in Peking. Many countries were not amused. In Brazil, the military government issued a ban on press reports of streaking, while the vice-president of Kenya warned that foreigners caught streaking would be deported, in the nude, on the first available aircraft.

Finding rhyme or reason to the fad was almost as popular as streaking itself. Some saw it as the sexual revolution manifest, others as an attack on dominant social values. The need for uninhibited reaction to months of gloom and doom on the newsfront was cited. But most simply regarded streaking as the latest rite of spring on college campuses. "It makes the world safe for goldfish," said Paul Bohannon, an anthropologist at Northwestern.

By late May, there was more streaking, but less attention being paid to it. Americans had had enough in the buff. Dr. Joyce Brothers reasoned that streakers had run out of ways to amaze, amuse, or startle onlookers. With that, streaking had run its course.

PET ROCK®

Frank White, 1985

Pet Rock®

145

The audacity of peddling worthless rocks in fine stores for $4 apiece! The NERVE of the guy behind the Pet Rock® craze of 1975!

But it was just preposterous enough to work. The sheer lunacy of owning a servile and faithful clump of stone so amused over 1.2 million Americans that they cheerfully parted with their money.

Pet Rocks® were the ultimate gimmick, a sedentary joke that came in a box with airholes and a wacky care and training manual. At the height of the fad—just before Christmas, 1975—entrepreneur Gary Dahl (pictured with a friend) was selling tens of thousands a day through the nation's most prestigious retail houses. They sold out everywhere, picking up momentum with a publicity ground swell in early fall that lasted well into 1976.

The thirty-eight-year-old unemployed advertising man from Los Gatos, California, got his flash of inspiration in a barroom one night. Friends were complaining about the high cost and headaches of pet ownership when Dahl remarked facetiously about his "pet rock."

His pet never soiled the carpet or clawed furniture, and it ate next to nothing. Friends unleashed a stream of one-liners, all very cute, about the eccentricities of domestic rocks. The concept was so ridiculous that Dahl began to take himself seriously. What if . . . Naw . . . But what if?

A crafty writer who once headed the creative department of a California ad agency, Dahl banged out a truly inspired care and training manual. It came out so well that he decided to package the idea. Dahl gathered a dozen or so smooth, egg-sized stones off the beach, had a friend design a quaint box for the pets, and then nestled them one by one in a fluff of straw.

In August 1975 he took his prototypes to the San Francisco gift show, where a buyer for Dallas's Neiman-Marcus department store saw them and ordered five hundred. More orders followed at San Francisco and at gift shows in New York and Los Angeles.

With orders to fill, Dahl began to look for financing. Several banks turned him down, but a friend in the ad business came up with $10,000 and America's next rock star was off and running. He bought two and a half tons of Mexican beach stones from a landscaping wholesaler and arranged to have them packaged at a local rehabilitation center for the physically and mentally handicapped. By early October he was turning out Pet Rocks.®

Neiman-Marcus had to reorder the same day they went on sale, and soon distinguished shops from around the country were asking for the peculiar product. Everywhere Dahl shipped them response was the same—stores couldn't stock his rocks fast enough.

But the big break came when he dropped off a press release at *Newsweek*'s San Francisco office. The magazine picked up on the boomlet and ran a story in its November 10 edition. What followed was an avalanche of media play.

Dahl did hundreds of interviews for newspapers, magazines, TV, and radio. He appeared on *Tomorrow* with Tom Snyder, the *Merv Griffin* show, and was a guest on *The Tonight Show* twice.

Dahl's manual was most of the fun. For example, he advised owners how to handle an excited rock when first brought home. "Place it on a newspaper," he wrote. "The rock will know what the paper is for and require no further instructions." Rocks could be taught to roll over, especially on hillsides, and they were particularly adept at heeling and playing dead. Guard rocks could be concealed and unleashed on attackers. The manual instructed owners to "reach into your pocket or purse as though you were going to comply with the mugger's demands. Extract your Pet Rock®. Shout the command ATTACK! and bash the mugger's head in."

Critics called it frivolous merchandising at its worst—a sad commentary on American taste. But Dahl figured the success of the rock was all in good fun. After Vietnam and Watergate he felt the country needed a laugh.

"People were tired of all the gloom," said Dahl near the end of the craze. "They wanted a good laugh. And the media were looking for a happy story, too; that's why I got all the publicity. Every TV station needed a brightener to put on after the weather."

A month after Christmas Dahl was still selling over fifteen thousand rocks a week, and pocketing ninety-five cents on each one. Less than a year after skimping along on his wife's earnings as a cocktail waitress and substitute teacher, he emerged a millionaire. By early 1976 he had bought a huge hillside mansion with an Olympic-sized pool, where he lazed and contemplated his rocky road to fortune.

Dahl earned more by licensing such Pet Rock® offshoots as Pet Rock® Food (rocksalt) and Pet Rock® Shampoo (an ordinary detergent). In November of 1976, a Florida State University child development professor tried to wean consumers off Pet Rocks® by marketing what he called Pet Ropes. They were three-foot strands of cotton, priced at $1 each, that were supposed to stimulate young children.

Most of the licensed by-products and competitors did poorly compared with the rock itself. But long after the fad died there were still attempts to cash in on an old joke.

In the fall of 1978, a California entrepreneur opened a five-hundred-acre rock resort where aging Pet Rocks®—for $5 a week—could lounge around a pool, go horseback riding, take nature hikes, and attend rock dances. There was also a training kit, with a tiny whip, to get the pet in shape for summer vacation.

Dahl had his own ideas after Pet Rocks® tumbled out of fashion in the spring of 1976. His Sand Breeding Kits consisted of male and female vials of sand that when mated could produce landfills, deserts, and cat litter. They did well at first, then tailed off after fifty thousand or so sold for $4 apiece.

He next tried marketing one-inch cubes of dirt allegedly smuggled out of Communist China. But the "Red China Dirt" joke collapsed when President Jimmy Carter formally recognized the People's Republic of China a few days after the product was introduced.

His new novelties never attracted much more than a brief media headturn. But no matter for Dahl, who eventually returned to the ad business—with his name on the door of a San Jose agency.

He had carved a small niche in history as the man who made millions selling Pet Rocks®. But more important, he was the guy who helped revive America's sense of humor.

MOOD RINGS

If there was a telltale artifact of the self-obsessed seventies it was probably the mood ring, a wildly popular trinket that was said to reflect the wearer's state of mind.

The famous ring consisted of special heat-sensitive liquid crystals encased in clear quartz that were engineered to change color with each minor fluctuation in body temperature. Different shades blazoned different feelings, or so the story went. Deep blue was blissful, reddish brown gave away insecurity, and so on down the psycho-chromatic scale.

Millions of Americans slipped them on during the summer

and fall of 1975 in a national show of emotion. They paid $250 for mood stone rings set in 14-karat gold and shelled out as little as $2 apiece for plastic stones set in fake gold.

Whether you were hot under the collar or playing it cool, the real mood stone made it public. The ring could sing your blues or show joy to the world. It was ideal for "getting in touch with your feelings," a favorite pastime of the seventies.

Before the jewelry tomfoolery subsided other psychological sensors were thrown on the market. There were watches which changed faces with each emotional twist of the wrist, handbags with straps to detect a cold shoulder, and belt buckles to light up with your midriff crises.

Before the craze lapsed there were also mood shoes, mood T-shirts, and mood nail polish. F. W. Woolworth sold mood panties, which featured small plastic hearts containing the liquid crystals.

Lord of the rings was a thirty-three-year-old New Yorker named Joshua Reynolds, a descendant of the great eighteenth-century British painter of the same name, and an heir to the R. J. Reynolds tobacco fortune. He created and marketed the original mood stone ring as an offshoot of Q-Tran Limited, a sensitivity body control training center he operated in Manhattan for the anxiety-ridden.

Using what the brochure described as "Liquid Color Crystals," Reynolds developed his "portable biofeedback aid." The idea was to make people more aware of their own emotions and learn to make positive mental adjustments.

To get his ring off and running, Reynolds hired a press agent, Valerie Jennings, who helped line up actress and perfume executive Polly Bergen as a major investor. Syndicated society columnist Eugenia Sheppard soon picked up word of mouth and wrote about the ring, and when they went on sale at Bonwit Teller in the summer of 1975, two local television stations covered the event.

Eight hundred of the $45 oval design rings set in sterling silver or vermeil were sold at the Bonwit jewelry counter within a few days of their introduction. In short order—and short supply—they turned up at Saks Fifth Avenue, Bloomingdale's, B. Altman & Company, and Bergdorf Goodman, creating a frenzy everywhere and touching off a national mood ring mania. Q-Tran sold $1 million worth of rings within three months but was soon lost in the shuffle and eventually went bankrupt.

An estimated three dozen manufacturers jumped in while Reynolds sought a patent as the original mood ring developer. Imitations were sold as the Impulse Ring, Personna Ring, and as Caprice and Tattletale stones. The copies generally sold for less, and some plastic versions made to look like the real thing could be purchased for loose change.

Another ringleader was the Michigan-based Gasco Company, which was shipping four thousand to six thousand a week during the fall. Owner Jack Tann sold his rings with a lifetime guarantee, even though everyone agreed the liquid crystal treatment would last only two to five years and then turn everlasting black. Tann figured the mood ring craze would be stone-dead after Christmas, and that a few years hence no one would care enough to press for a refund.

But for the time being mood rings were red hot. An estimated fifteen million were sold by December 1975, outpacing such previous fads as Indian jewelry, copper bracelets, and love bracelets with throwaway keys.

Owners included celebrities Muhammad Ali, Joe Namath, Paul Newman, Valerie Perrine, Steve McQueen, Barbra Streisand, and Sophia Loren, whose ring turned bad news black during a press conference and became the focus of front page stories the next day. Loren was such a mood ring fanatic that she bought one hundred from Dallas's Neiman-Marcus department store and had them shipped to Italy.

Reynolds's brochure included a color key. Various shades of felicitous blue showed everything from quiet ease to ecstasy. Jade green meant the wearer was active, but not under stress. Yellow revealed a lack of focus, and reddish brown pegged you as out of sorts. Black was worst of all, proclaiming the subject "tense, inhibited, harassed." But it could also mean the wearer was cold, since a chill in the air caused the stone to darken.

The lingering question was whether the mood stone actually did as purported. Could the clear quartz stone paint an emotional portrait from its palette? Scientists who pondered the ring suggested that liquid crystals worked in the same way as a digital thermometer, activating at precise temperatures. In fact, crystals had long been used by doctors to identify varying skin temperatures. Some experts finally gave it the benefit of the doubt. After all, the hands and feet did indeed suggest emotional conditions, as exemplified by the cold, clammy hands of nervous people.

Mood ring inaccuracy made for popular banter at the height of the fad. Lots of wearers had stories—an employee hounded by the boss while the ring shone a contented azure, or a happy reveler looking down on a blackened stone. But millions took their cue from the hue.

Ultimately, the search for scientific truth seemed irrelevant, since buyers believed what they wanted. Furthermore, the fad's six-month run was hardly long enough to conduct a great debate on mood ring reliability. Once the bauble built momentum there was no cause to doubt its authenticity. The mood ring was a raging novelty, a must to own whether it displayed emotion or the time of day.

When enthusiasm for mood rings began to ebb in 1976, not even a glowing endorsement in the *New England Journal of Medicine* would have helped. Sales fell off dramatically and the mood stone could not say why. There was no color in its spectrum for boredom.

CB RADIO

Camerique

Equipped with citizen band radio kits and a rich slanguage popularized by truckers, Americans in 1976 turned themselves into a huge network of ratchet-jawing "good buddies."

A quiet corner of the airwaves, set aside nearly thirty years earlier for noncommercial public use, was transformed into the hottest new communications forum since television. An estimated twenty-five million CB sets were sold in the bicentennial year—enough to suddenly crowd channels with a nonstop chatter that could be lifesaving or mindlessly shrill.

More than a radio frequency, CB was an underground culture that came to the surface. With its own mother tongue—a colorful and creative jargon honed on the highway—CB was a netherworld of fast-talking bliss.

It was first used to shake truckers from boredom and sleep and spread warnings about radar-bearing highway patrolmen. But at the peak of the fad even First Lady Betty Ford was a CB owner, calling out "breakers" from the White House under the handle "First Mama."

CB seemed more than just another craze, given the enormous practical applications of two-way radio. Road emergencies could be communicated rapidly, and travelers could receive traffic information. The Chrysler Corporation predicted that by 1979, 80 percent of all new models would come equipped with CB, and some electronics industry analysts felt they would someday be as commonplace as television sets.

But when the novelty faded, CB radio was exposed as an electronic toy. Sales plummeted in 1977 and fell even further the next year. Meanwhile, citizen band channels cleared up almost as fast as they had been overrun.

The tiny radio band was opened by the Federal Communications Commission in 1947 for the short-range use of private citizens. It was intended to be a communication link for persons who either lived, worked, or recreated in areas without access to telephones.

But with federal imposition of the fifty-five miles per hour national speed limit in 1973, truckers began using CB channels extensively. The two-way, twenty-three channel receivers and transmitters, which ranged four or five miles, were used to call out the movements and whereabouts of police officers.

Media attention magnified the folksy, southern-bred trucker lingo and the CB craze took off. Between the time the first license was issued in 1947 and the rise in truck driver use twenty-five years later, about eight hundred fifty thousand licenses were granted by the FCC. But by mid-1976, applications were pouring in at the rate of six hundred fifty thousand a month. The FCC's CB office in Gettysburg, Pennsylvania, was literally flooded with paper as requests for licenses spilled into the ladies room.

Sales volume for CBs went through the roof—reaching an

estimated $1 billion in 1976. A bevy of small manufacturers leaped into the business ahead of the large manufacturers and cleaned up. A typical success story was Xtal Corp, a Northridge, California, company that began in a one-room office in 1973 and saw sales climb to well over $10 million in both 1975 and 1976.

The early twenty-three channel sets ranged in price from under $100 for one that could be installed in a car, truck, or boat, and powered by a vehicle battery, to over $700 for a sophisticated home-based system. Through the first six months of 1976 manufacturers had trouble satisfying demand, because of limited plant capacity and a shortage in the world supply of the natural quartz used for radio crystals. Retailers waited months for shipments while customers were placed on hold.

But even persons without CB radio could not avoid the sudden infatuation with trucker talk. Down-home, good ol' country gear-jammer phraseology crept into conversations nowhere near a CB radio and far from the Deep South. The "breaker, breaker" call, used to initiate CB transmissions, was a national catchphrase, and "that's a 10–4, good buddy" became the universal affirmative.

More than terminology, CB language was a colloquial state of mind one adopted behind the wheel. The fifty-five miles per hour speed limit translated as "double nickels," police officers were "Smokey Bears," "Smokies," or just "bears," and nontruckers occupying the road were "cotton pickers."

To keep up with the vernacular, Americans bought hundreds of thousands of CB jargon dictionaries. The chatter was so widespread that a few academics worried about permanent damage being done to the English language, noting that CBers concerned themselves more with flashy imagery than good grammar.

Besides hot-selling CB glossaries, the craze manifested in other ways, including several B-films that inevitably pitted laidback good buddy haulers against sniveling Smokies. Country singer C. W. McCall's smash hit record *Convoy* was a trucker saga told in CB-ese, while the television series *Movin' On* also glorified the over-the-road gang.

While CB was an empty-headed diversion for some practitioners, a spate of serious-minded clubs sprang up to relay road emergencies. The largest was REACT (Radio Emergency Association Citizens Team), which formed in 1962 but saw membership swell to over seventy thousand nationwide when the CB fad took hold in 1976.

The surge of citizens band broadcasting brought over-the-air headaches for the FCC, including reports of solicitation by prostitutes, mounting use of obscenities, and such a serious crowding of channels that in heavily populated areas, transmissions sometimes blended together to become one continuously garbled and unintelligible drone.

Some CB radios leaked signals, causing interference with other electronic devices. There was growing frustration with rambling CB monologues that suddenly invaded public address systems, overwhelmed television reception, confused traffic lights, and caused automatic garage doors to open by themselves.

As part of the solution, in mid-1976 the FCC began working on a plan to increase the number of available CB channels from twenty-three to forty, a shift also seen as a potential marketing bonanza for manufacturers and retailers.

But just as the federal agency began taking steps to open the airwaves, the CB radio fad began to fade out. Companies riding a crest in early summer had to revise projections drastically when sales slipped in July and slowed considerably by fall.

When forty-channel sets hit the market that winter, retailers found surprisingly little interest. Stores canceled orders and began clearing out remaining twenty-three channel stock at cut-rate prices. Makers closed plants and scrambled to diversify in the electronics field.

Truckers kept on transmitting after everyone else signed off. But few hard-driving white-liners would be caught dead mouthing the CB clichés they originated.

RUBIK'S CUBE®

Rubik's Cube® is a registered trademark of CBS, Inc., and is used by its permission.

Rubik's Cube®

Americans began toying with Rubik's Cube® in 1980 and for the next year or so could hardly put the baffling geometric puzzle down.

The Cube was a sort of national intelligence test that got twiddled and thumbed for hours on end, only to be thrust vehemently aside and picked up again, moments later, for still more pawing and piddling. It was hard to solve but even harder to ignore.

By the end of 1981 over ten million manic obsessives the world over had measured their I. Qube on the three-dimensional riddle, and most came away feeling sadly outclassed.

Hungarian architectural professor Erno Rubik concocted the puzzle in 1974 as a mental exercise for his students. He assembled a six-sided cluster of cubelets, with each facade showing nine colored squares set in rows of three. The rows could be rotated in any direction by 360 degrees, which allowed the configuration to be radically altered with a few twists and turns. When taken out of the box, Rubik's Cube® bore a solid color on each side. The object was to realign the colors after they had been scrambled.

It was no easy trick, not when it was possible to arrange the Cube in any one of 43,252,003,274,489,856,000 different patterns. Yet some managed to do it with amazing ease. At the height of the fad, a sixteen-year-old British high school student solved the puzzle in twenty-eight seconds. He was part of an international cult of cubists who increased their speed by disassembling the puzzle and lubricating the moving parts so they could be twiddled more rapidly.

Another measure of prowess was the number of moves it took to finish. A British mathematician successfully completed the puzzle in fifty moves, but it was a calculated and deliberate exhibition rather than a show of speed.

Though the cube could be mastered, most owners remained thoroughly puzzled—laboring for days, weeks, even months while never able to arrange more than one side as a solid block of color. Some fingered the plaything absentmindedly while engaged in conversation or watching television. But others fell into rapt concentration and shut out the world.

Stories of cube compulsion began turning up in the media. There was the woman who needed an operation for tendonitis of the thumb because she fidgeted with the toy so much. Another woman sued for divorce, citing her husband's infatuation with the Cube, to the exclusion of all marital attentions, as the root of their incompatability.

A few years after the fad subsided, Rubik himself theorized on the magnificent obsession. "It is a trap and it is quite easy to walk into," he said. "It looks quite harmless. But once you get hold of it, it affects your self-esteem, vanity. You figure so many others have done it, children, and you tell yourself you're not more stupid than they are."

An entire industry grew around the panicky need to solve the puzzle. Two books, *The Simple Solution to Rubik's Cube*® by James Nourse and *Mastering Rubik's Cube*® by Donald Taylor, became runaway best sellers. Some fifty books for Cube strategists were eventually put into print, but there were no easy solutions. Some books advocated convoluted theories that even surpassed the puzzle for befuddlement.

For those who could do the puzzle well, there was competition for prize money. Meanwhile, the Museum of Modern Art in New York saw beauty in the beast and placed the toy in its permanent design collection.

The fad even drew comic backlash. Two California entrepreneurs marketed the "ultimate solution," a plastic paddle called "Cube Smasher" that could be used to demolish the puzzle. The pair quickly sold more than one hundred thousand smashers as frustration mounted.

Of course, the Cube itself was a sales sensation. Ideal Toy Company sold four and a half million worldwide in 1980 at $6–$10 retail, after obtaining a license from a Hungarian state-owned manufacturer to manufacture the product. Sales reached the ten million mark by the end of 1981, while twice as many counterfeit cubes sold at far below the price of the authentic Rubik's Cube.® Ideal sued more than twenty American firms in 1981 for importing illegal versions from foreign countries.

Sales of the Cube began to level off in 1982, but Ideal was

already back on the market with spin-off puzzles. Rubik developed "The Magic Snake,®" a geometric brain twister that could be worked into various shapes. Other companies brought out variations of the Cube, challenging players to match colored squares or arrange them in patterns.

Rubik continued to hatch new puzzles, such as a four-row version of the original called "Rubik's Revenge.®" But though offshoots sold well for a time, Rubik and his imitators could never match the intoxicating appeal of the Cube. The toy had made him a millionaire many times over, but he eventually returned to teaching at the university-level Academy for the Applied Arts in Budapest. "Everyone expects something better," he said. "But I'm not a toymaker. How can I top the Cube? It's a terrible problem."

PAC-MAN™

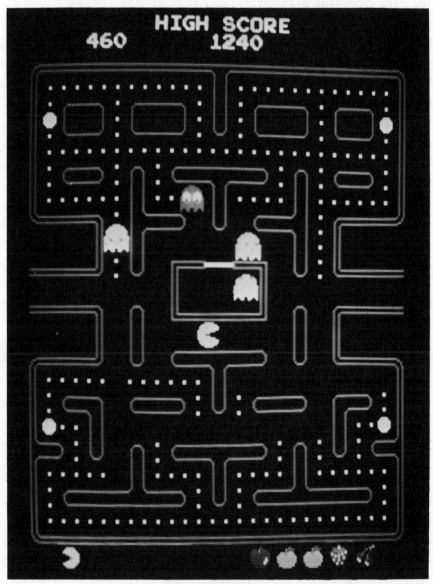

Pac-Man™

Pac-Man,™ the first great hero of the video game wars, looked like a souped-up Smile Button when he arrived on the screen in 1981. He was a mellow yellow peril, a happy-go-lucky omnivore who starred in his own computer game and became a powerful symbol of the 1980's.

Pac-Man's™ arcade fame was enormous and immediate, touching off a tidal wave of merchandising in 1981 and 1982. The Great Gobbler turned up on over two hundred consumer products via lucrative licensing deals and even landed a Saturday morning cartoon series.

By early 1982, the coin-operated Pac-Man™ game was already waning in popularity in video halls. But there was enough excitement left over to keep retailers busy selling everything from home screen versions of the arcade game to sherbet bars shaped like Pac-Man.™

Namco Limited, a Japanese computer and robotics firm, developed the game in the 1970's. The character was based on a Japanese folk hero with a legendary appetite and derived its name from the word *paku,* meaning to eat. The U.S. rights were acquired in 1980 by Bally Manufacturing Company, and it was introduced in video parlors early the next year.

The response from arcade players was phenomenal. In 1981, Bally sold ninety-six thousand coin-operated games at about $3,000 each; Pac-Man™ surpassed Space Invaders as the most popular quarter slot in the country. The game swallowed up an estimated $1 billion in loose change within eighteen months to far outdistance the revenue garnered by such other youthful diversions as "Star Wars" and "Raiders of the Lost Ark."

Pac-Man™ roamed through his electronic maze with mouth ajar, ever ready to devour the dots and colorful fruit he chased. The more Pac-Man™ could pack away, the more points a player guiding his movement accumulated. Meanwhile, Pac-Man™ sought to avoid four ghosts in the machine, The Galaxians, who could eat or be eaten by the hero.

Pac-Man™ on a video screen was a national intoxicant for

both kids and adults, and the game proved to be the first arcade hit with women. Sociologists reckoned it was because Pac-Man's™ victims were quickly and mercifully digested, not blown from the sky with video weaponry.

The desire not only to play Pac-Man™ but play it well, became an obsession with the young. Word of record scores spread through arcades like wildfire. Guidebooks titled *How to Win at Pac-Man™* and *Mastering Pac-Man™* turned up on national best-seller lists. *People* magazine staged a celebrity Pac-Man™ contest and drew more than forty Hollywood stars, most of them young television performers who had grown up with joystick in hand.

The tremendous arcade exposure made the Pac-Man™ character a natural in other consumer markets. Bally moved fast on the licensing front, signing up dozens of Pac-Man™ offshoot makers and splitting up the proceeds with Namco. The list of products included lunch boxes, pajamas, blue jeans, watches, mugs, clocks, greeting cards, gift wrapping, sheets and pillowcases, children's clothes, breakfast cereal, ice cream, and dozens of toys.

Besides the Saturday morning cartoon series, Pac Mania also spread to the radio. Jerry Buckner and Gary Garcia released an album called *Pac-Man™ Fever* on Columbia Records and saw the title song crack *Billboard* magazine's Top 10.

Atari Division of Warner Communications struck a deal directly with Namco to produce a home video cartridge version of the arcade game. Atari scheduled introduction of the game, which listed at $37.95, around a Pac-Man™ publicity blitz in April and a massive television advertising campaign.

Coleco Industries, a major figure in the handheld computer game binge of the late seventies, contracted with Bally to market a six- by eight-inch battery-operated tabletop Pac-Man™ game. Milton Bradley weighed in with a non-electronic board game based on the arcade Pac-Man™, along with a card game and Pac-Man™ puzzle.

Bally found yet another gaming angle to the craze by introducing a Pac-Man™ pinball set in April. It was an ironic attempt to spur sales of pinball machines which had slumped badly while in competition with electronic games.

Pac-Man™ moved out of the arcades and into home computer game systems just as it was becoming stale in fad-oriented video halls. But a few months later the booming cartridge market suffered a serious downturn.

Despite its home version of Pac-Man,™ Atari faltered in the fourth quarter of 1982. The once soaring electronic game giant, and other industry leaders, was beset by an explosion of competition. The blazing home video game business had been doused. After forecasting a drop in fourth quarter earnings, Warner's stock dropped a full nineteen points during a seven-day span in December 1982.

Even the introduction of Ms. Pac-Man™ on the home amusement front could not prevent the market from receding after a long stretch of undisturbed growth. But by that time the Pac-Man™ visage—the "Mickey Mouse of the eighties" as one Bally executive described it—was established, especially with small children who related to the bubbly cartoon figure, if not the video game from whence it came.

With product licensing appeal intact, Pac-Man™ was not about to pack it in. Kids would be sleeping on Pac-Man™ bed sheets and eating Pac-Man™ cereal for years to come.

SMURFS™

It took twenty-five years for the Smurfs™ to go from the sketch pad of Belgian illustrator Pierre (Peyo) Culliford to the lunch pails, knapsacks, wading pools, and transistor radios of millions of American children.

But when Culliford's cuddlesome blue gnomes finally caught on in this country, they caught fire. They became superstars of the character licensing game that dominates child product marketing in the United States.

Smurfs™

165

The Smurfs,™ who according to their legend stand "three apples high" and live in Smurf-ect harmony amid an enchanted forest, performed a miracle of merchandising in 1982. A deep-blue sea of Smurf™ goods washed over retail America that year, and the company holding U.S. licensing rights pegged sales at about $600 million.

Smurfees Law: Whatever can be licensed, will be.

Conceivably, kids could surround themselves with Smurf-things from the time they popped out of a colorful Smurf™ bedsheet and ate a bowl of Smurf™ breakfast cereal until they cleaned their teeth at night with a Smurfbrush, kicked off Smurf™ slippers, and jumped back into a blue-and-white bed.

Culliford's Disneyesque pixies, who wear identical white stocking caps, were created for a children's book in 1957. European toy companies were soon turning out dolls and other items based on the characters, which took on names like Lazy, Greedy, Brainy, and Jokey Smurf. The lone female member of the happy clan is Smurfette, and the elves are gently supervised by the wise and bearded Papa Smurf.

The characters became *Die Schlümpfe* in Germany, *Smolf* in Scandinavia, *Los Pitufos* in Spain, and *I Puffi* in Italy. They gained gradual acceptance on the Continent until, in 1978, British Petroleum launched a promotional campaign based on the creatures.

England was overwhelmed by "Smurfanalia." It began with distribution of T-shirts, posters, and figurines at filling stations and culminated with a recording, "The Smurf™ Song," which ascended the British pop charts.

Mindful of their popularity overseas, Wallace Berrie, a U.S. company selling stationery and ceramic statues bearing happy homilies, obtained a license to Smurf™ in America.

Columbia Pictures previously held the U.S. rights, but made little effort to market the Smurfs™ here. Wallace Berrie, on the other hand, moved quickly after gaining licensing privileges. The firm began with two-inch figurines, which sold briskly on impulse racks for $1.50 apiece and then looked for ventures with other manufacturers. Within a year the company had signed up more than a dozen sub-licensees, and the groundwork was set for Smurfin' USA. Among the big name participants were Mattel, Coleco, Milton Bradley, Mead, and Catalina.

The big break was NBC's decision to air a regular cartoon series on Saturday mornings. Although the network once rejected a Smurf™ show, legend has it that NBC president Fred Silverman became enthusiastic when daughter Melissa fell in love with the little trolls. Silverman commissioned Hanna-Barbera, creators of *The Flintstones* and countless other animated children's series, to produce a Smurf™ program.

Although Silverman was soon ousted, the Smurfs™ became a Saturday sensation with small children. The show helped boost NBC from last place to first in the Saturday morning ratings and was soon increased in length from thirty minutes to ninety minutes.

The program became The Smurfs'™ central showcase and a launchpad for Wallace Berrie's ambitious marketing plans. The company continued to produce Smurf™ dolls itself but sold sublicenses for a galaxy of Smurf™ articles that included video games, vanity sets, plastic pedal cars (Smurfmobiles, of course), clocks, eating utensils, stickers, and all manner of toys and children's clothing.

Of course, if you're winsome, you lose some. There were a few cries of Smurf™ overkill beginning in late 1982 by critics who felt small children were getting too much of a cute thing. Some complained that Smurfs™ were without substance—either literary or legendary—and got by on adorability alone.

Hanna-Barbera portrayed the Smurfs™ as magical little people with an all-for-one and one-for-all spirit. In saccharin-sweet cartoon episodes, they learned lessons in good Smurf™ citizenship—taught to be elfish not selfish—or fended off the evil forays of Gargamel the magician, their archenemy. In between time they "la la la" the nonstop Smurf™ melody as though distant cousins of the Seven Dwarfs.

So successful were the Smurfs™ that in the year of *E.T.,* they walloped Steven Spielberg's extraterrestrial superstar on the marketing front. They also outsold the Star Wars characters, Strawberry Shortcake, Garfield, Snoopy, Annie, The Dukes of Hazzard, and Mickey Mouse—all licensing favorites.

The Smurf™ clamor quieted some in 1983, but the merchandising tide continued to roll, and the band of blue fairyfolk seemed destined to survive. Like the ageless Disney characters and long-lasting comic strip heroes, the Smurfs™ were settling into a niche, preparing to charm succeeding generations of preschool youngsters.

CABBAGE PATCH KIDS™

They looked something like the young actor who played Larry Mondello on *Leave It to Beaver*. With cheeks fat and floppy, lips pursed, nose pinched and eyes aglaze, Cabbage Patch Kids™ were the perfect come-hither dolls. And they were sewed up in a spongy skin that made them more caressable than dolls molded out of cold, hard plastic.

Each was given a name pulled from 1938 Georgia birth records and packaged with a set of "adoption" papers. And thanks to computerized factories, no two Kids were alike.

In fact, Cabbage Patch Kids™ were quite unlike any doll in history when they arrived in 1983, and they got a reception like none other. America was heartsmitten. A nation of children wanted them to have and to hug.

Cabbage Patch Kids™ became the hottest store-bought

babykin since Raggedy Ann. In the weeks before Christmas, 1983, demand reached an impossible fever pitch. Baby bedlam was everywhere. Competition for Kids even turned ugly as jostling, grabby shoppers engaged in one department store fracas after another.

At a discount house in Wilkes Barre, Pennsylvania, one woman suffered a broken leg when she was caught in the midst of a thousand shoppers who'd waited eight hours to get at the dolls. As the mob advanced, a department manager took up a baseball bat to hold his ground. At a hobby shop in Middletown, Connecticut, buyers waited ten hours for twenty-four dolls delivered by armored car. Uniformed guards, with side arms, kept the peace.

The manager of a Best Products store in Dallas was threatened by angry shoppers who pushed their way into the store's receiving bay. The rabble demanded that he break Cabbage Patch Kids™ out of crates and sell them on the spot.

Fearing a riot, the manager of an F. W. Woolworth in Lawrence, Kansas, put the store's last seven dolls in a bank vault and held a drawing for the rights to buy them. The owner of the Merry-Go-Round Toy Discount Center in New Rochelle, New York, where police were needed to control a Cabbage Patch crowd, told a reporter, "I've never seen a fad like this, not even Hula Hoops."

The most famous incident involved a Milwaukee radio station which facetiously broadcast that two thousand dolls would be tossed out of a B–29 circling over County Stadium. Buyers needed only hold up American Express cards for photographing from the air. Two dozen gullibles, with eyes fixed skyward, showed up in bitter cold for the great Cabbage Patch drop.

To avoid such nonsense, a Shawnee, Kansas, letter carrier flew to England to find a Cabbage Patch doll for his five-year-old daughter. A London newspaper bought him five dolls in exchange for an exclusive interview.

One woman "adopted" ninety-seven dolls at a cost of $2,425. Forty-eight Cabbage Patch Kids™ were stolen from the home of a Holland, Michigan, woman. State police troopers found them stuffed into five plastic garbage bags left in a trash bin at a nearby park.

The Cabbage Patch crop grew out of the fertile mind of a young Georgia sculptor named Xavier Roberts. After discovering similar soft sculptures at art and craft fairs in the South, he begat his own baby in 1977. Roberts stitched together a soft torso and limbs, plugged the navel, attached yarn tresses and created that face . . . that fabulous face. He puckered up his plumpkins, recessed their chins, inflated their jowls, and then dimpled his dollies. With arms outstretched and eyes wide with wonderment, they were pure inanimate magnetism.

Roberts formed Original Appalachian Artworks to turn out diapered "Little People" by hand in a converted medical clinic in Cleveland, Georgia, dubbed Babyland General Hospital. Roberts was the hospital's "chief of staff." Employees—the famous "folks at the Cabbage Patch"—wore hospital garments while bringing new dolls into the world.

An ingenius marketing ploy had much to do with the Little People's regional success. Buyers, who laid out $125 for original Cabbage Kids from Babyland General, went through an "adoption" ritual, pledging to love and care for the dolls. Eventually, two hundred fifty thousand were "placed through adoption," and the originals were soon fetching up to $1,000.

Cabbage Patch Kids™ were brought to mass market by Coleco Industries, the giant toymaker which began life in the 1930's as the Connecticut Leather Company. Coleco had been in the middle of a raging fad before, having cleaned up with Davy Crockett moccasin kits in 1955.

The company took shrewd control of the new doll after it was passed over by the likes of Fisher Price and Mattel. It manufactured a sixteen-inch, $25 version of Roberts's handmade dolls, replacing the cloth face with vinyl skin.

Coleco retained the "adoption" ploy, enclosing a realistic "birth certificate" and adoption papers which asked "parents" to raise their right hand in front of another person and say, "I promise to love my Cabbage Patch Kid™ with all my heart. I promise to be a good and kind parent. I will always remember how special my Cabbage Patch Kid™ is to me." Each doll came with a card describing "my special personality traits." A typical one read "I'm very shy but once you get to know me I'll tell you more about me."

The colorful Georgia names were part of the charm. They came with monikers like Clarissa Sadie, Barnaby Billie, Cornelia Lenora, and now and then a plain Mary Stephanie.

According to "The Legend," as conveyed by Coleco on a card strapped to each doll's wrist, "Many years ago a young boy named Xavier happened upon an enchanted cabbage patch where he found very special little people who called themselves Cabbage Patch Kids.™'" Xavier "set out in search of parents to adopt them—a search that will continue as long as there are children looking for love."

Like Original Appalachian Artworks, Coleco managed to make each doll a little different from the rest. Assembly lines were programmed to vary clothes, skin tone, hair color, the turn of the mouth, dimples, freckles, and other attributes.

Coleco aimed high, lining up a bevy of Hong Kong manufacturers, testing the market extensively, and stoking enthusiasm among high-powered retailers.

The dolls were a hit at the February 1983, New York Toy Fair, where Coleco piled up enough orders to guarantee a successful debut for its Kids. Then came a series of public relations masterstrokes, including endorsements from Dr. Joyce Brothers and other psychologists, a mass adoption ceremony at the doll's formal introduction in June, numerous magazine mentions, a long segment on NBC's *Today* show and, finally, an old-fashioned run on the product.

Unsure about overall retail sales prospects, department stores ordered modestly at first. But it turned out shoppers were rushing Christmas, 1983. Coleco's production sources, which consisted of eight factories grinding away in the Far East, were straining to keep up.

Jetliners brought back two hundred thousand dolls a week from the Orient. Emery Worldwide, the air freight company called on to speed deliveries to the States, ran ads heralding its Cabbage Patch connection. The company boasted that "to keep up with these kids you've gotta be fast."

But Coleco was still falling behind, and the shortages did even more to fuel the national obsession. There were orders for the entire original capacity of two million dolls by early October. The company geared up for production of hundreds of thousands more by Christmas. But when December 24 rolled around, Cabbage Patch Kids™ were still the rarest of items, selling for well over list price when available. Many were bought and sold by independent scalpers who hawked their wares in department store parking lots for $100 and up.

Coleco officials finally estimated that 3.2 million dolls were sold in 1983, and six months into 1984, 2 million more were delivered.

But even while shoppers clamored for the dolls, they remained puzzled by their attraction. "Why all the commotion?" went the refrain. "They're sooooo ugly!" For months, ugly was the issue. Dr. Joyce Brothers surmised that "it is comforting to feel the Cabbage Patch doll can be loved with all your might—even though it isn't pretty." But Cabbage Patch Kids™ grew on America . . . and fast. They became merely homely. Then cute. Then adorable. Then irresistible.

Soon the vegetots were everywhere. And there were countless accessories—including several clothing combinations, strollers, cribs, slumber bags, and carriers—followed by countless items licensed to bear the famous Cabbage Patch kisser. Within a few months of the first department store frenzy, there were Cabbage Patch books, records, roller skates, pedal cars, luggage, games, puzzles, powder puffs, musical swings, and virtually anything else appealing to the juvenile set.

It was a licensing extravaganza to match the Smurf,™ Strawberry Shortcake,™ and Pac-Man™ phenomena. Toy stores were all but made over in the ubiquitous green and yellow Cabbage Patch color scheme. There were the doll spin-offs from Coleco, the infantile Preemies,™ the Wykoosa Valley™ Koosa™ pets, and Cabbage Patch miniatures.

Next came the imitations—cheaper and by the dozens. A new generation of dolls eschewed the prim Barbie look and took on plump Cabbage Patch proportions. Among the lookalikes were Flower Kids, Pumpkin Kids, Love Me Dolls, Blossom Babies, and Cauliflower Babies, who wore an Italian knit outfit and came out of their own plastic "cauliflower." Ads for some dolls boasted that "we wear Cabbage Patch clothes." Roberts took a few imitators to court, charging some manufacturers with counterfeiting and others with copyright infringement.

The Kids loosed some creative offshoots. Lots of Cabbage Patch "parents" sent "kids" to Camp Small Fry—started by Dr. Sanford Stein of Rumson, New Jersey, to prove that children treated the dolls as if they were children of their own.

On San Francisco's trendy Union Street, a former Coleco marketing vice-president and his partner opened a store called The Doll Patch, selling nothing but Cabbage Patch Kids.™ The Doll Patch charged about twice as much as most retail outlets for Kids. But customers lined up anyway because they could get them without spending weeks on a waiting list. The owners hired theater students dressed up in surgical garb and nurses' uniforms to stage delivery and adoption rituals for customers. "Parents" also received a photograph of the ceremonies.

As with any mania, there came controversy. Coleco had promised to send "first birthday" cards to owners, but volume was so great that getting them off on time proved all but impossible. The Detroit-based Adoption Identity Movement called Cabbage Patch Kids™ a "degrading, offensive and dehumanizing exploitation of the adoption process." Nonetheless, several hospitals agreed to give blank certificates of adoption to anyone who wanted them for any kind of doll. In February 1984 the Social Security Administration warned state agencies to watch for fraudulent welfare applications based on the certificates. A hospital in California had a day when kids could bring their "kids" in for vaccinations.

The golden tykes had become a daily news event. Everyone, everywhere, was talking them up. Cabbage Patch Kids™ had seeped into the American mainstream.

While destined to slip quietly out of the limelight, they had already grabbed a piece of history. They would be remembered by new generations of youngsters as the perfect model to coddle.

Also available from Quill

What We Wore
An Offbeat Social History of Women's Clothes, 1950 to 1980
Ellen Melinkoff

Combining social history with women's archetypal recollections, this book looks at what we wore, where we wore it, what people said about it, and most important, how we felt about it.
0-688-02228-6

How Do They Do That?
Wonders of the Modern World Explained
Caroline Sutton

How do bees build honeycombs? How are tunnels dug underwater? This book entertainingly unravels some of the modern world's greatest puzzles—a browser's delight.
0-688-01111-X

How *Did* They Do That?
Wonders of the Far and Recent Past Explained
Caroline Sutton

From How did they get the stones in place at Stonehenge? to How did Superman fly in the movies? and over 100 other classic curiosities.
0-688-02230-8

AT YOUR LOCAL BOOKSTORE